TOP SHELF
SEASONAL SAMPLER 2008

TOP SHELF PRODUCTIONS publishes contemporary graphic novels and comics by artists of singular vision. Dedicated to championing veteran creators as well as finding and developing emerging talent, the Top Shelf library is anchored by such masters of the craft as Alan Moore (*FROM HELL*, with Eddie Campbell; *LOST GIRLS*, with Melinda Gebbie), Craig Thompson (*BLANKETS, CARNET DE VOYAGE*), Andy Runton (*OWLY*), Jeffrey Brown (*CLUMSY, UNLIKELY*), Alex Robinson (*BOX OFFICE POISON, TRICKED*), James Kochalka (*AMERICAN ELF, SUPERF*CKERS*), Robert Venditti (*THE SURROGATES*, with Brett Weldele), Jeff Lemire (*ESSEX COUNTY*), Matt Kindt (*SUPER SPY*), Renée French (*THE TICKING*), and many more.

Known for excellent production values, our handsomely crafted editions combine the best in reproduction techniques with a unique, inspired design sensibility. Never limiting ourselves in format or content, our catalogue includes all-ages material and cutting-edge erotica, genre fiction and autobiography, and all that exists in between. The recipient of dozens of awards, we continue to bring superior stories and ideas to the ever-growing audience of the comics medium.

The Top Shelf brand stands as a hallmark of quality — a fine addition to any connoisseur's library.

Art from *That Salty Air*, Tim Sievert.

www.topshelfcomix.com

Art from *Swallow Me Whole*. Nate Powell.

TOP SHELF
SEASONAL SAMPLER 2008

EDITS. CHRIS STAROS
DESIGN. CHRIS ROSS & BRETT WARNOCK
COVER. JEFF LEMIRE. BACK COVER. MAX ESTES
INSIDE COVERS. TIM SIEVERT
FACING IMAGE. NATE POWELL

FEATURING THE WORKS OF:

J.D. Arnold	Pat Mills
Corey Barba	Alan Moore
Jeffrey Brown	Steve Moore
Eddie Campbell	Scott Morse
Lilli Carré	Kevin O'Neill
David Chelsea	Nate Powell
Nikki Cook	Liz Prince
Jon B. Cooke	Brian Ralph
Kristian Donaldson	Aaron Renier
Ray Fawkes	Alex Robinson
Renée French	Andy Runton
Melinda Gebbie	Wayne Shellabarger
Rob Goodin	Pete Sickman-Garner
Andy Hartzell	Tim Sievert
Ulf K.	Christian Slade
Bill Kelter	Chris Staros
Matt Kindt	Craig Thompson
James Kochalka	Jeremy Tinder
Rich Koslowski	Robert Venditti
Jeff Lemire	José Villarubia
Vince Locke	Brett Weldele
Nicolas Mahler	Brian Wood
Lars Martinson	David Yurkovich
Kagan McLeod	Aleksandar Zograf

TOP SHELF PRODUCTIONS
PORTLAND/ATLANTA

Art from *Too Cool to Be Forgotten*. Alex Robinson.

ISBN: 978-1-60309-032-2

Top Shelf Seasonal Sampler 2008 © and ™ 2008
Top Shelf Productions, Inc. All featured works
and sample artwork © 2008 the respective
writers and artists. Published by Top Shelf
Productions, PO Box 1282, Marietta GA
30061-1282, USA. Publishers: Brett Warnock
and Chris Staros. Top Shelf Productions® and
the Top Shelf logo are registered trademarks
of Top Shelf Productions, Inc. All Rights
Reserved.

First Printing, Spring 2008.
Printed in Canada, by Lebonfon.

TABLE OF CONTENTS

Perennials...

APPENDICIES

Art from *Owly: A Time to be Brave*. Andy Runton.

FINDING TOP SHELF PUBLICATIONS

FANS

Top Shelf publications are available, or can be ordered from, wherever graphic novels and books are sold. To find a particular title, ask your local comic book retailer or bookstore to order a copy. If you don't know where the nearest comic book shop is, you can use the free comic shop locator service by calling 888.COMIC.BOOK (888.266.4226) or visiting the website: http://csls.diamondcomics.com/. If there isn't a comic shop or bookstore near you, then you can visit www.topshelfcomix.com.

WHOLESALE DISTRIBUTION FOR RETAILERS

BOOK TRADE

Top Shelf publications are distributed worldwide to the book trade by Diamond Book Distributors (DBD), and are also available from Ingram, Baker & Taylor, Bookazine, Partners West, Brodart, Follett, and other wholesalers through DBD.

Bookstores can contact DBD here:

DIAMOND BOOK DISTRIBUTORS
1966 Greenspring Dr Ste 300
Timonium MD 21093
USA
410.560.7100 (secretary) x 840
410.560.7112 (automated / after hours) x 840
410.560.2583 (fax)
dbd@diamondbookdistributors.com
www.diamondbookdistributors.com

DIRECT MARKET ——————————————————————————————
Top Shelf publications are distributed to the direct market by Diamond Comics Distributors,
Last Gasp, and Top Shelf. Comic book retailers can contact our distributors here:

DIAMOND COMICS DISTRIBUTORS
1966 Greenspring Dr Suite 300
Timonium MD 21093
USA
800.45.COMIC (customer service)
410.560.7100 x 215 (new accounts)
www.diamondcomics.com

LAST GASP
777 Florida St
San Francisco CA 94110
USA
800.366.5121
415.824.6636
415.824.1836 (fax)
www.lastgasp.com
Sales Reps:
Kristine Anstine, kristine@lastgasp.com
Jon Longhi, jon@lastgasp.com
Jeri Rossi, jeri@lastgasp.com

TOP SHELF PRODUCTIONS
PO Box 1282
Marietta GA 30061-1282
USA
770.427.6395 (fax)
Chris Staros, chris@topshelfcomix.com
Brett Warnock, brett@topshelfcomix.com
Robert Venditti, rob@topshelfcomix.com
www.topshelfcomix.com

2008 RELEASES

Here's everything Top Shelf has planned (so far!) for 2008. Do yourself a favor this year and try something you're not familiar with. You won't be disappointed.

ALL-AGES TITLES

OWLY & FRIENDS (FCBD). Runton, Slade, Kochalka, and Barba
OWLY (VOL 4): A TIME TO BE BRAVE. Andy Runton
OWLY (VOL 5): TINY TALES. Andy Runton
KORGI (BOOK 2): THE COSMIC COLLECTOR. Christian Slade
JOHNNY BOO (BOOK 1): THE BEST LITTLE GHOST IN THE WORLD.
JOHNNY BOO (BOOK 2): TWINKLE POWER. James Kochalka
YAM. Corey Barba

MATURE TITLES

Welcoming…
THAT SALTY AIR. Tim Sievert
SWALLOW ME WHOLE. Nate Powell
TONOHARU: PART ONE. Lars Martinson
HIERONYMUS B. Ulf K.
VEEPS. Bill Kelter & Wayne Shellabarger
CRUM BUMS. Brian Ralph
24x2. David Chelsea

From the veterans…
TOO COOL TO BE FORGOTTEN. Alex Robinson
ESSEX COUNTY (VOL 3): THE COUNTRY NURSE. Jeff Lemire
SULK. Jeffrey Brown
DELAYED REPLAYS. Liz Prince
AMERICAN ELF (BOOK 3). James Kochalka
LITTLE PAINTINGS. James Kochalka
COMIC BOOK ARTIST (VOL 2) #7: THE PETER BAGGE ISSUE.
COMIC BOOK ARTIST (VOL 2) #8: THE TONY HARRIS ISSUE.

2008 ALL-AGES TITLES

OWLY & FRIENDS
Andy Runton, Christian Slade, James Kochalka, and Corey Barba
32-Page Comic Book
UPC Code: 094922892386
Absolutely Free on Free Comic Book Day
Dimensions: 6 5/8" x 10 3/16"
All Ages

Top Shelf kicks off its all-ages releases for the year with the 2008 FREE COMIC BOOK DAY comic book, *OWLY & FRIENDS*. In this FCBD edition, we're not only presenting an all-new Owly adventure by Andy Runton, but also three other all-new, all-ages adventures from Owly's friends: Korgi by Christian Slade, Johnny Boo by James Kochalka, and Yam by Corey Barba. This comic book is perfect for everyone in the family and is a great way to keep up with *OWLY* and *KORGI*, as well as get introduced to Top Shelf's two new 2008 all-ages series, *JOHNNY BOO* and *YAM*.

FREE AT YOUR LOCAL COMIC BOOK RETAILER ON MAY 5TH —
FREE COMIC BOOK DAY!

OWLY (VOL 4): A TIME TO BE BRAVE
Andy Runton
128-Page Graphic Novel
ISBN 978-1-891830-89-1
$10.00 (US)
Dimensions: 5 1/4" x 7 1/2"
All Ages

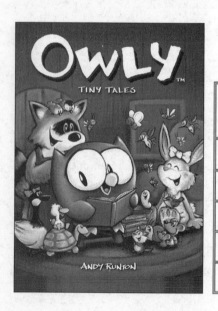

OWLY (VOL 5): TINY TALES
Andy Runton
144-Page Graphic Novel
ISBN 978-1-60309-019-3
$10.00 (US)
Dimensions: 5 1/4" x 7 1/2"
All Ages

"The adventures of this little 'bird of play' will charm readers of any age."
—Erik Pedersen, E! Online

"It's a beautiful, touching entrée that grabs and holds the heart and makes one smile."
—Jeannine Wiese, Ingram Library Services

"Charming ... reminiscent of children's "literature in the style of Frog and Toad, or Winnie the Pooh and Piglet."
—Publisher's Weekly

The fourth graphic novel in the amazing all-ages *OWLY* series, *A TIME TO BE BRAVE*, tells the story of a new visitor to the forest. He may be misunderstood because of how he looks, but things aren't always what they seem, and everyone soon finds out that the power of friendship can fix just about anything. And the fifth graphic novel, *TINY TALES*, kicks off with a brand new Owly adventure, and also collects the very first out-of-print Owly stories from the original mini-comics, as well as the out-of-print Free Comic Book Day stories "Splashin' Around," "Breaking the Ice," and Helping Hands." Other bonus materials in Volume 5 include a Sketchbook Section as well as a "How To Draw Owly" Section. Both graphic novels are the perfect way to complete your *OWLY* collection and make sure you have every Owly story ever told on your bookshelf. Relying on a mixture of symbols, icons, and expressions to tell his silent stories, Andy Runton's clean, animated, and heartwarming style makes it a perfect read for anyone who's a fan of Jeff Smith's *Bone* or Dave Pilkey's *Captain Underpants*. Don't miss the latest big thing in graphic novels!

Andy Runton is the creator of the breakout all-ages series of graphic novels, *OWLY*, starring a little owl who's always searching for new friends and adventure. In addition to winning the Eisner, Harvey, and Ignatz awards, as well as the Howard E. Day Memorial Prize, his work has garnered praise from such high-profile publications as *People*, *Publishers Weekly*, and *USA Today*. After only a few years on the comics scene, Andy already shines as one of the industry's brightest stars. He currently resides in the greater-Atlanta area, where he's working full-time on the next *OWLY* graphic novel.

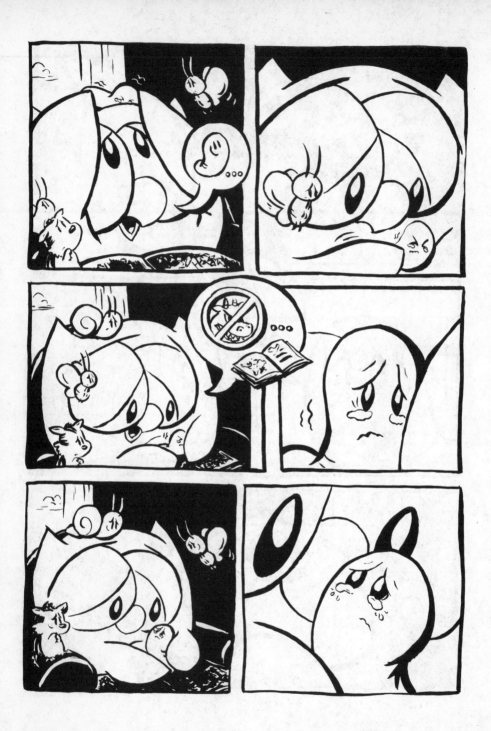

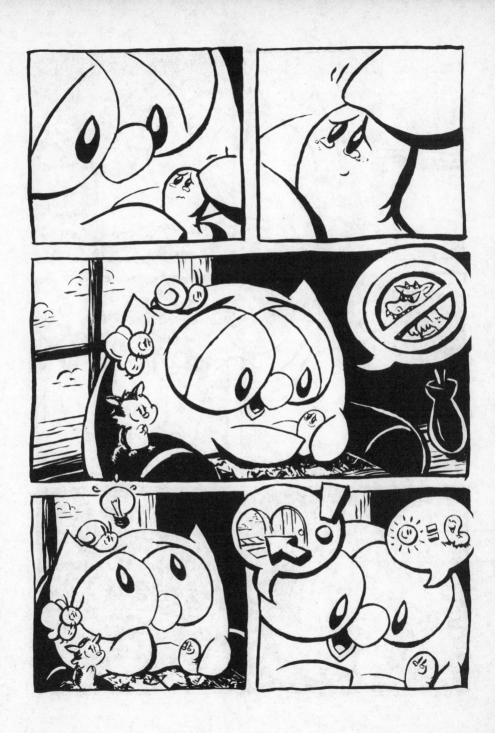

KORGI (BOOK 2): THE COSMIC COLLECTOR
Christian Slade

88-Page Graphic Novel
ISBN 978-1-60309-010-0
$10.00 (US)
Dimensions: 6 1/2" x 8 1/2"
All Ages

"Once you pick up KORGI, *if you have a heart, you will not be able to put it down or stop going 'That's so cute!!!'"*
—The Beat/Publisher's Weekly

THE COSMIC COLLECTOR is the second volume in the critically acclaimed, all-ages graphic novel series, *KORGI*. In this volume, things are not going too well in Korgi Hollow. While a mysterious hunter has trapped and clipped the wings off of many mollies, Ivy and Sprout search for answers in the surrounding woods … but they may be facing something that is totally out of this world! *KORGI* is a gorgeously illustrated woodland fantasy perfect for fans of J.R.R. Tolkien or Andy Runton's *OWLY*.

As a boy growing up in New Jersey and carrying his sketchbook with him wherever he went, it was said that Christian Slade sometimes lived in another world. It was this other world within the pages of his sketchbook that made him obsessed with drawing from his imagination and the world around him. After 30 years, not much has changed. Christian lives in Orlando, Florida with his wife Ann, their new twins, and their two Welsh corgis Penny and Leo.

JOHNNY BOO (BOOK 1): THE BEST LITTLE GHOST IN THE WORLD
James Kochalka

40-Page Full-Color, Hardcover Graphic Novel
ISBN 978-1-60309-013-1
$9.95 (US)
Dimensions: 6" x 9"
All Ages

JOHNNY BOO (BOOK 2): TWINKLE POWER
James Kochalka

40-Page Full-Color, Hardcover Graphic Novel
ISBN 978-1-60309-015-5
$9.95 (US)
Dimensions: 6" x 9"
All Ages

"Kochalka's command of the comic form is sublime and adorable. Kids will love JOHNNY BOO."
—*Harry Bliss,* Diary of a Worm

Johnny Boo is the best little ghost in the whole world, because he's got Boo Power. This means that he can go "BOO" really loudly. His pet ghost named Squiggle has Squiggle Power, which means that he can fly and do really fast loop-the-loops. Together they have the world's greatest ghost adventures! They enthusiastically frolic and roughhouse, having ghost races and drinking melted ice cream, but they often accidently hurt each other's feelings, and have to comfort and console one another. In Book 1, when the giant pink and yellow Ice Cream Monster bumbles into their lives, they go into a mad panic… until they discover that he's actually quite friendly. In Book 2, Squiggle goes on a quest to learn the secret of twinkle power from the twinkling stars, but doesn't have much luck. Instead, a strange and hilarious secret is discovered about Johnny Boo's hair. Both books will have the kids howling with laughter.

James Kochalka is, without question, one of the most unique and prolific alternative cartoonists working in America today. His comics have been published internationally by nearly every alternative comics publisher; he's recorded several music CDs (for Ryko) under the name James Kochalka Superstar (making him a favorite at college radio stations across the country); and he's developed animated cartoons for Nickelodeon. Best known for his graphic novel *MONKEY vs. ROBOT,* his comic book series *SUPERF*CKERS*, and his critically acclaimed diary strip *AMERICAN ELF*, James currently lives in Burlington, Vermont with his wife Amy, kids Eli and Oliver, and cat Spandy, all of whom are often characters in his comics.

"Hey James, how did JOHNNY BOO *come to be?"*

"I sketched one chapter at a time, and tested them out on my 3-year-old son as bedtime stories," says Kochalka. "If he didn't laugh really hard, I went back and rewrote the chapter and tried again, until the story was honed to perfection. So, there's at least one little boy in the world for which this story is incredibly, hilariously funny. I think that lots of other kids will probably have a similar reaction."

"As a kid myself, I was in love with comics and children's books. I loved Dr. Seuss's strange creatures. My favorite book of all was *The Bad Island*, by William Steig. It was scary and sad and funny and beautiful, and best of all it had incredible monsters of every shape and size. I've been drawing unusual creatures of my own design ever since. *Casper the Friendly Ghost* was also a pretty obvious influence, especially for the cuteness factor of my drawing. Even my experience watching 70s television sitcoms like *Three's Company* were a big influence on *JOHNNY BOO* with its looping, crazed misunderstandings and manic energy."
—James Kochalka

CHAPTER ONE

YAM
Cory Barba

88-Page Graphic Novel
with a full-color section

ISBN 978-1-60309-014-8

$10.00 (US)

Dimensions: 6 1/2" x 9"

All Ages

Top Shelf is proud to present an all-new, "silent" all-ages graphic novel series … Yam and his fun-loving friends live on the remote tropical island of Leche de la Luna, and are always getting mixed up in surreal adventures. Whether it's encountering cupcakes that spring to life, befriending potted flowers, or exploring the mysterious ruins on the island, this small boy in his hooded, footy pajamas always ends up having a blast with his friends. The debut graphic novel, simply titled *YAM*, is anchored by the full-length story "Toy with My Dreams," in which Yam develops a crush on a girl much too old for him, but ends up being able to communicate with her in his dreams. The graphic novel also contains a full-color section and several short stories which have seen print in *Nickelodeon Magazine*. Sure to be a real treat for anyone who's a fan of *OWLY* or *KORGI*.

Chicago-area native Corey Barba is an animator, illustrator, cartoonist, and musician. He's been creating kid's comics for *Nickelodeon Magazine* for the last 8 years, and underground comics for much longer. His work has been published by Fantagraphics Books, the online humor magazine *Tastes Like Chicken*, in various comic anthologies, and was shown in the Pictoplasma Book and exhibition.

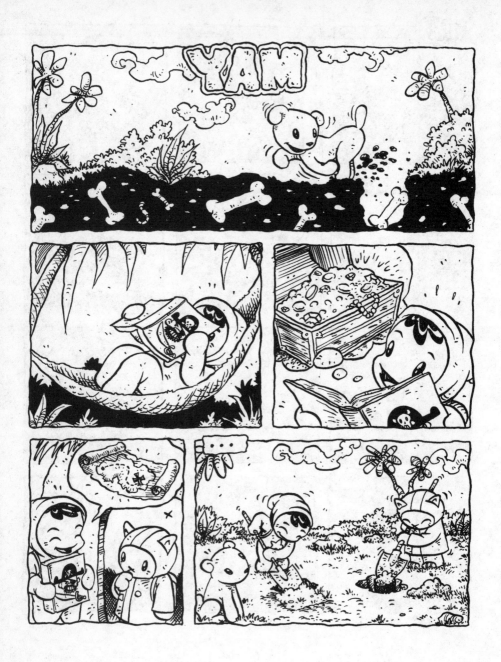

2008 MATURE TITLES

PLEASE JOIN US IN WELCOMING THE FOLLOWING CARTOONISTS & PROJECTS TO THE TOP SHELF FAMILY THIS YEAR…

THAT SALTY AIR
Tim Sievert
112-Page Graphic Novel
ISBN 978-1-60309-005-6
$10.00 (US)
Dimensions: 6 1/2" x 9"
Mature (13+)

Hugh is a fisherman with a special relationship to the sea, a relationship based on respect and reverence. But when Hugh feels that the sea has betrayed him, his whole existence is thrown out of whack. Hell-bent on settling the score, Hugh takes his revenge to the extreme, jeopardizing not only himself, but also his family in the process. *THAT SALTY AIR* is a story about change and learning the price for trifling with the natural progression of things.

Tim Sievert was born in Davenport, Iowa, on April 12, 1983. At the tender age of nineteen, he was shipped away to Minneapolis, Minnesota, where he currently lives and works in the wonderfully hectic world of interactive media. In his off hours, Tim works so extremely hard on his comics that you wouldn't even believe it.

SWALLOW ME WHOLE
Nate Powell

216-Page Graphic Novel
ISBN 978-1-60309-033-9
$14.95 (US)
Dimensions: 6 1/2" x 9 1/2"
Mature (16+)

"A cartoonist's cartoonist, Powell employs stunning technique in some of the most complex, elusive stories in the comics medium... Frame by frame, his work is more varied in every way than that of most other comics artists, yet he unfailingly maintains narrative momentum by carrying over details from one panel to the next, no matter how altered the angle of vision. Brilliant.
—Ray Olson, Booklist

SWALLOW ME WHOLE is a love story carried by rolling fog, terminal illness, hallucination, apophenia, insect armies, secrets held, unshakeable faith, and the search for a master pattern to make sense of one's unraveling. Two adolescent stepsiblings hold together amidst schizophrenia, obsessive compulsive disorder, family breakdown, animal telepathy, misguided love, and the tiniest nugget of hope that the heart, that sanity, that order itself will take shape again.

Nate Powell wakes up before sunrise most days in his home of Bloomington, Indiana. He hails from North Little Rock, Arkansas, a beautiful, dried-up place where he began publishing in 1992 at the age of 14. In recent years he has created the *Walkie Talkie* series, *Tiny Giants*, and *It Disappears* for Soft Skull Press; *Sounds of Your Name* for Microcosm Publishing; and most recently *PLEASE RELEASE* under the Top Shelf banner. Since 1999, Nate has also worked full-time doing support and care work for folks with developmental disabilities. To boot, he wiggles in the bands Soophie Nun Squad and Wait, squanders petroleum products with the Harlan Records label, and cries waaaaay too easily when watching movies. Nate packed a sack lunch every day in high school.

| **TONOHARU: PART ONE** Lars Martinson |
| 128-Page, Two-Color Hardcover Graphic Novel |
| ISBN 978-0-9801023-2-1 |
| $19.95 (US) |
| Dimensions: 5 1/2" x 8 1/4" |
| Mature (16+) |

Top Shelf is proud to distribute the Xeric Award-winning graphic novel from Lars Martinson. With amazing production values and a layered and cross-cultural storyline, this book is sure to make a mark on the comics community.

Daniel Wells begins a new life as an assistant junior high school teacher in the rural Japanese village of Tonoharu. Isolated from those around him by cultural and language barriers, he leads a monastic existence, peppered only by his inept pursuit of the company of a fellow American who lives a couple towns over. But contrary to appearances, Dan isn't the only foreigner to call Tonoharu home. Across town, a group of wealthy European eccentrics are boarding in a one-time Buddhist temple, for reasons that remain obscure to their gossiping neighbors … A 128-page, hardcover graphic novel with a full-color dust jacket and two-color interiors.

Lars Martinson was born on Mother's Day, 1977. He has met a princess, seen a five-legged cow, and eaten raw octopus eggs. From 2003 to 2006 he taught English in Fukuoka, Japan through the Japan Exchange and Teaching Program. In 2007 he received the prestigious Xeric Grant for his graphic novel *TONOHARU: PART ONE*. He currently lives in Minneapolis and is hard at work on the second part of the Tonoharu story.

I live in the sticks. The nearest real city is an hour away and the trains going there stop early.

My little town has its charm, but cosmopolitan it ain't. I am currently the only non-Japanese resident.

A family from Eastern Europe used to live here for some reason, but they left a few months before I got here.

From the sound of it, they didn't make too many friends. The events surrounding their departure are still discussed in hushed tones.

The only expat I ever met in my neck of the woods didn't seem like he'd win too many popularity contests either.

It was about a week after I arrived. He had been working as an AET a few towns down the line.

I asked if he had any insights for someone new to the job. His response was light on advice and heavy on anger and self-pity.

Every word out of his mouth was dripping with venom. Japan was shit, his job was a joke, all the other teachers were incompetent jerks…

Granted, his situation did sound pretty dismal. His predecessor broke her contract and left several months early, leaving behind loose ends and bitter colleagues.

In any case, I was quick to dismiss him. He was just an asshole that was using Japan and a crappy job as scapegoats for his own issues.

After listening to him for forty minutes, we finally got to my stop and I could make my escape. I never saw him again.

I still suspect my knee-jerk assessment of him was more right than wrong, but since then my own experience has made me a little more sympathetic.

Sometimes it feels like the AET program was designed to ensure discontent. There's the countless hours of idle time…

The geographical remoteness, the language barrier, the thousand little cultural differences…

Allow all this to stew for a few months without an outlet for release, and it's enough to drive anyone a little crazy.

Sometimes I wonder if it's just a matter of time before I become that guy on the train, spewing bile at whoever is unfortunate enough to cross paths with me.

But I don't want to paint too bleak a portrait of life here. There's plenty to be thankful for, too.

Harro, harro!

There's my students. Mister Sato. The food. High-tech toilets. The drunken reverie of the teacher parties, where the language barrier temporarily becomes a non-issue.

Getting to see the Spring Festival floats alone would have made everything else worth it.

And actually, every experience I've had here, even the unpleasant ones, have deepened my understanding both of myself and of the wider world.

I feel privileged to have had the opportunity. In no way do I regret spending a year here.

If I was sure I'd see improvement in just a few key areas, I'd renew my contract in a heartbeat.

But if a second year was just more of the same, then the law of diminishing returns would apply and it would be a waste of time.

As much as I hate to admit it, I think the second scenario is more likely. I've worked myself into a pretty deep rut.

But the idea of giving up just rubs me the wrong way. My foolish pride tells me to struggle on, consequences be damned!

The question is, is it still possible to turn things around? Or would I just be wasting a year to satisfy my ego?

I only have a few days to decide, and frankly, I have no idea what I'm going to do.

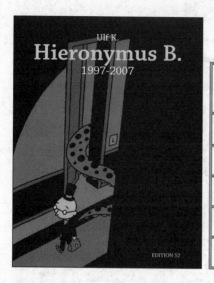

Ulf K.
Hieronymus B.
1997-2007

EDITION 52

HIERONYMUS B.
Ulf K.

64-Page Hardcover Graphic Novel
ISBN 978-1-60309-008-7
$14.95 (US)
Dimensions: 5 1/2" x 7 1/2"
Young Adult (13+)

Top Shelf is proud to be one of the five international publishers simultaneously releasing *HIERONYMUS B.*, the all-new hardcover graphic novel from the award-winning German cartoonist, Ulf. K. Ulf is best known for his endearing silent stories, and this graphic novel — featuring tales of the loveable and humble clerk, Hieronymus B. — will charm anyone. Ulf K. has been illustrating the (silent) tales of Hieronymus B. for ten years now, and it's time that the American comics audience got a glimpse of what this amazing cartoonist has been up to.

Ulf K. was born in 1969 in Oberhausen, Germany, right in the heart of the Ruhrgebiet. It was there, in the shadows of the blast furnaces, that he spent his childhood and adolescence, as well as studied graphic design at the University of Essen. In 1996, he was briefly pulled to Paris, but became so homesick that he quickly fled back to the shade of his beloved blast furnaces. Today the artist lives with his family in Düsseldorf. In 2004, Ulf K. was awarded the Max and Moritz Prize as Best German-Language Cartoonist at the International Comic Salon in Erlangen.

| **VEEPS** |
| Bill Kelter & Wayne Shellabarger |
| An Election Year Spectacular! |
| 180-Page Illustrated Hardcover |
| ISBN 978-1-60309-003-2 |
| $19.95 (US) |
| Dimensions: 5 5/8" x 8 1/2" |
| Mature (16+) |

It's a tired but true cliché that every American Vice President is just a heartbeat away from the most powerful job in the world — a job they've often never really interviewed for. Who are these people? We all know about the one who shot his hunting partner in the face, but how about the tavern owner who once married one of his slaves and then sold her at auction when she tried to leave him? Or the one whose President went to his death regretting that he hadn't had his Vice President hanged? Or the one who was too frequently inebriated to serve out the whole of his term? Over more than 200 years, the American voters have sent a platoon of rogues, cowards, drunks, featherweights, doddering geriatrics, bigots, and atrocious spellers to Washington D.C. to sit one bullet, cerebral hemorrhage, or case of pneumonia away from the highest office in the land. *VEEPS* tells the sordid, head-scratching, perversely-entertaining stories of these men we've chosen to ride shotgun in the biggest rig in democracy, without ever seriously considering the possibility that they might have to take the wheel.

Bill Kelter is a part-time writer and full-time "Internet something-or-other" as his friends and family would say of his vague occupation. He enjoys fine barbecue, the occasional cold beverage, and his several televisions, which he keeps on most days in hopes that he might catch a political or entertainment luminary doing something foolhardy and career-destroying, or hear O. J. Simpson finally confess, just so he can say he saw it live. He lives in Vancouver, Washington.

Wayne Shellabarger lives and works in San Francisco. He is currently listening to a Bo Diddley record. His previous publication with Top Shelf was a collection of rock posters he drew for The Cherry Poppin' Daddies, called *I'M TOTALLY HELPLESS*, one of Top Shelf's very first publications.

John Adams

Thomas Jefferson

Lyndon B. Johnson

Gerald Ford

AARON BURR
DEMOCRAT-REPUBLICAN, NEW YORK
WITH THOMAS JEFFERSON, 1801–05

For most people, being second in charge of the newest, coolest country on Earth would be excitement enough. But, as John Adams discovered immediately and as most of his successors would as well, with this ostensibly great power comes no responsibility. Most wiled away their time attending the occasional meeting and special event, and aging in dog years waiting for one of the least-eventful episodes in their career to come to a merciful end. Between accusations of his complicity in the 1800 electoral vote tie which very nearly won him the Presidency over Thomas Jefferson, and the tumultuous state of his personal and financial affairs that kept him away from Washington much of the time, Burr's term in office was anything but uneventful. Even still, he seemed to have bigger itches to scratch in his life. His taste for adventure helped him become the only sitting Vice President to be charged with murder and former VP to be charged with treason.

"PRESENT ARM!":

When Burr held a command at Valley Forge, one cold night a mutiny was stirring during roll call. A soldier drew a pistol at an unsuspecting Burr and called to his fellow troops, "Now is your time boys!" But Burr would brook no coup on his watch. He deftly drew his sword and, with one swipe, hacked off the man's arm, ending the insurrection as quickly as it had begun.

> *"I never, indeed thought him an honest, frank-dealing man, but considered him as a crooked gun, or other perverted machine, whose aim or stroke you could never be sure of.."*
> – Thomas Jefferson on his former Vice President. Coming from a man as intellectually uncomplicated as Jefferson, the gun reference was surely unintentional.

An effective display of leadership? Certainly, but it's hard to imagine a youthful Walter Mondale ever dismembering someone for challenging his authority.

HAMILTON BREACHED

Alexander Hamilton and Burr tolerated one another at best. The history between the men was already dicey. Burr in 1800 hijacked an anti-John Adams pamphlet authored by Hamilton, which embarrassed Hamilton and, upon Jefferson and Burr's electoral tie, prompted him to lobby Congress to award the Presidency to Jefferson, which they ultimately did. After the 1804 gubernatorial election, Hamilton got his drink on at a dinner party and expounded at length against Burr's fitness as a man and a public figure, calling him "a dangerous man...who ought not to be trusted". Burr was outraged when the comment was widely repeated and reprinted, but Hamilton refused to apologize. Their war of words escalated until Burr challenged Hamilton to the 19th century equivalent of duking it out in the parking lot.

The two nemeses met bright and early on July 11, 2004 at the dueling grounds in Weehawken, New Jersey, where young men today are still duking it out in parking lots over petty personal slights. Hamilton got off the first shot, but missed. Burr's .54-caliber ball ruled the day, finding its mark and exacting a gruesome toll on Hamilton's groin and internal organs, and he died the next day. History has done a much more devastating number on Burr's legacy, thanks in large part to the duel, but in fairness to the much-maligned Vice President, it was discovered when the pistols were donated many years later to the Smithsonian Institute that Hamilton's had been secretly modified to enable a quicker discharge. Unfortunately, Hamilton appears to have leaned a bit too heavily on the trigger and fired early. The wages of cheating perhaps.

FREE BURR

Burr had one of the more interesting lame-duck periods in the history of his office. Besides being charged with murder in New York & New Jersey, Burr began work on building his own empire across part of Mexico and the

Spanish colonies of the American Southwest. He even negotiated (while still in office) a meeting with the British minister to the United States to inquire if he would help procure funds for a war to help bring the territory under his control. He chose to stay on the move, in part to pursue his Southwestern Dream, in part because of the sunshine and beautiful country down south, and in part because of the two murder warrants out for him.

Where best to hide but in plain sight? After an abortive trip to Mexico via Florida, Burr returned to finish his term as Vice President. Ironically, Washington D.C. was his safest bet to avoid arrest--the District of Columbia had no extradition agreement with the rest of the states.

GOLDEN YEARS

After leaving office, Burr's vision turned to a grandiose plan for American Revolution. Such incendiary talk understandably displeased the Presi-dent, and Burr was arrested in New Orleans and eventually charged with treason. Ultimately acquitted, Burr had to escape a tar-and-feather mob in Baltimore and angry creditors in Philadelphia, and would find safe accommodations in Europe (where he allegedly contacted Napoleon about a possible attack on Boston).

In his twilight, Burr found solace in letters and women, sending breezy notes to his beloved daughter, Theodosia, regaling her with tales of his favorite European prostitutes, rating them by price and satisfaction--the kind of bonding every daughter longs for from her father. He died on his 80th birthday--the same day his divorce was finalized.

He could find some solace in his posterity: In his lengthy official biography on the United States Senate Web site, the words "duel", "murder", and "treason" are nowhere to be found.

Fun Facts

As a young Lieutenant Colonel, Burr was made a member of General George Washington's Staff, but was transferred after Washington caught him reading the General's mail.

Burr would, later in life, use his mother's maiden surname, Edwards, as his birthname was inextricably linked with scandal and his considerable outstanding debts.

CRUM BUMS
Brian Ralph

| 208-Page Graphic Novel |
| ISBN 978-1-60309-002-5 |
| $15.00 (US) |
| Dimensions: 5" x 6" |
| Young Adult (13+) |

Brian Ralph began *CRUM BUMS* nearly ten years ago, and, even though there seemed little hope of this epic ever seeing print, Top Shelf was determined to get Brian to complete this long lost masterpiece. The wait is over, and we are finally able to put it on the schedule. A time traveling Monkey finds himself marooned in the future. With little hope of repairing his time machine, he wanders the barren post-apocalyptic landscape alone. But when he meets a curious group of future punks, it seems as though the future might not be as inhospitable as he thought!

Brian Ralph is an Illustrator and Cartoonist living in Baltimore whose work appears in various publications, most notably *Nickelodeon Magazine*. In addition, Brian has three published graphic novels, *Cave-In*, *Climbing Out*, and *Daybreak*. His comic strip "Reggie-12" ran in many issues of *Giant Robot Magazine* — check the robot archives at www.reggie12.com. Brian is a 1996 graduate of the Rhode Island School of Design with a BFA in Illustration, and from 1996–2000 he lived at the influential Fort Thunder warehouse. Brian currently teaches Sequential Art and Character Design in the Illustration Department at the Maryland Institute College of Art. *CRUM BUMS*, his latest work, will be his Top Shelf graphic novel debut.

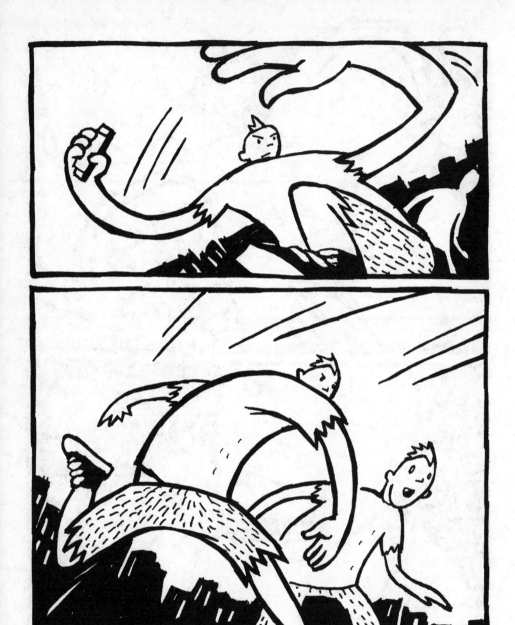

24x2
David Chelsea

48-Page Comic Book

UPC 094922897800

$5.00 (US)

Dimensions: 5" x 7 1/2"

Mature (16+)

"Twenty-Four Times Two." The author of *David Chelsea In Love* and *Perspective!* picks up Scott McCloud's ball and runs with it in these two 24-Hour Comics stories (out of a flabbergasting eight he's produced over the past few years). In "Everybody Gets It Wrong" David makes the argument that all autobiographical comics produced so far, definitely including his own, falsify experience because they show the author as one of the characters rather than telling the story as seen from his own eyes. Putting theory into practice, David illustrates a number of dreams from his diary while strictly keeping to the dreamer's point of view. "Sleepless" takes this method further, telling a richly stippled story of lava lamps, time travel, and a mysterious lady cartoonist in blue velvet, all seen through the eyes of a lead character who is never shown.

David Chelsea grew up in Portland, Oregon, and later moved to New York City for a spell. He is the author of the graphic novels *David Chelsea in Love* and *Welcome to the Zone*, as well as the instructional book *Perspective!: A Guide for Comic Book Artists*. His comics and illustration have appeared in numerous publications, including the *New York Times*, the *New York Observer*, and the anthology *TOP SHELF: ASKS THE BIG QUESTIONS*. He lives in Portland, Oregon.

EVERYBODY GETS it WRONG!

HARVEY PEKAR GETS IT WRONG!

ART SPIEGELMAN GETS IT WRONG!

NINA PALEY GETS IT WRONG!

EVEN THE GREAT CRUMB! WRONG! WRONG! WRONG!

i GOT IT WRONG!

WHAT'S WRONG WITH THIS PICTURE?

YOU'RE DUMPING ME? WHAT FOR?

①

THIS IS WHAT IT SHOULD HAVE LOOKED LIKE...

YOU'RE DUMPING ME? WHAT FOR?

WHO IS THIS IMAGINARY OBSERVER AND WHERE IS HE SITTING?

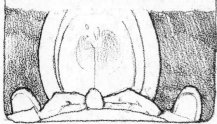

IF WE AUTOBIOGRAPHICAL CARTOONISTS REALLY WANT TO BE TRUE TO EXPERIENCE, SUBJECTIVE CAMERA IS THE ONLY WAY TO GO!

THINGS WOULD LOOK VERY DIFFERENT...

WILL YOU QUIT DRAWING FOR ONCE AND LOOK ME IN THE EYE?

ESPECIALLY SEX SCENES.

UHN! UHN!

I CAN UNDERSTAND IT— AUTOBIOGRAPHICAL CARTOONISTS DON'T WANT TO LIVE LIFE OVER EXACTLY— THIS TIME THEY WANT BETTER SEATS!

②

BY THE WAY, REMEMBER THE SCENE IN BEDAZZLED WHEN DUDLEY MOORE BECOMES A FLY ON THE WALL SO HE CAN SPY ON HIS GIRLFRIEND IN THE MORGUE?

THAT WAS COOL.

OK, BUT HERE'S WHAT THEY GET **REALLY WRONG**—

Dream Scenes!

QUESTION: WHEN YOU DREAM, DO YOU SEE YOURSELF?

I BET YOU DON'T!

SO WHY DOES EVERY DEPICTION OF A DREAM SHOW THE DREAMER?

③

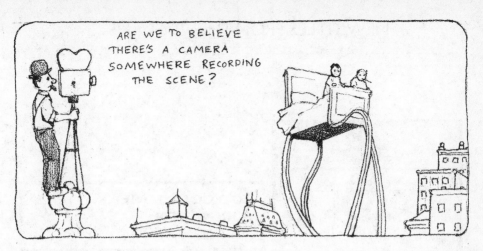

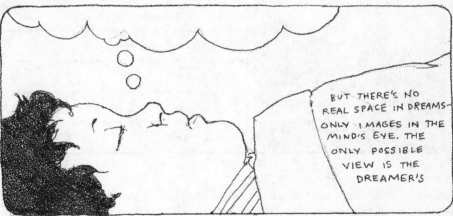

④

TOO COOL TO BE FORGOTTEN Alex Robinson
128-Page Hardcover Graphic Novel
ISBN 978-1-891830-98-3
$14.95 (US)
Dimensions: 5 1/2" x 7 1/2"
Mature (16+)

Andy Wicks is a forty-something father of two who's tried everything to quit smoking — from going cold turkey, to the latest patches and nicotine chewing gums — so he figures he'll give this hypnosis thing a try. What's the worst that could happen? Unfortunately, Andy gets dealt a fate worse than death — high school! Transported back to 1985, Andy returns to his formative years as a gangly, awkward teenager. Is he doomed to relive the mistakes of his past, or has he been given a second chance to get things right? One thing's for sure - this time he's going to ask out that girl from math class… Presented as a gorgeously formatted hardcover graphic novel.

Alex Robinson graduated from Yorktown High School in 1987. He worked in a major metropolitan bookstore for seven years before finally quitting to draw comics full time. His Top Shelf books include the award-winning graphic novels *BOX OFFICE POISON* and *TRICKED*, as well as the short story collection *BOP! [MORE BOX OFFICE POISON]* and the barbarian farce, *ALEX ROBINSON'S LOWER REGIONS*. He lives in New York City with his wife, Kristen, and their two cats, Cadbury and Krimpet. He divides his time between dusting his collectible gaming miniatures and chastising himself for not working more.

"YOUNG MAN?" THAT'S FUNNY. OKAY, I'LL PLAY ALONG:

I'M JUST GOING TO THE BATHROOM, MR. MARKSTEIN. I'LL BE RIGHT OUT, I PROMISE.

ANDY, A PASS NEXT TIME, OKAY? OR I'LL SHOW YOU WHAT REAL BALL BUSTING IS.

MOZART MC WOWS KICKS!

YOU GOT IT. AND THANKS A--

BOY

OH, UH, HEY, FELLAS. I WAS JUST TALKING TO MR. MARKSTEIN OUT THERE.

I HOPE I'M NOT INTER--

WAS HE TELLING YOU HOW GOOD YOUR NUT-SACK TASTED LAST NIGHT?

PHAHAHA!

GRATEFUL

WHOA! HAHA, OKAY, LET'S TONE IT DOWN A NOTCH, OKAY? YOU--

YEAH, I HEARD HE GAVE YOU FIFTY BUCKS TO LET HIM GIVE YOU A BLOW JOB AT DOWNING LAST NIGHT.

Cape Cod

WH--?? YOU GUYS DON'T EVEN KNOW ME. WHAT THE HELL IS YOUR--

SURE I KNOW YOU. WE'RE IN THE SAME GYM CLASS YOUR NAME IS GAYLORD, RIGHT?

YEAH, GAYLORD QUEERBAIT, RIGHT?

ESSEX COUNTY (VOL 3): THE COUNTRY NURSE

Jeff Lemire

| 128-Page Graphic Novel |
| ISBN 978-1-891830-95-2 |
| $9.95 (US) |
| Dimensions: 6 1/2" x 9" |
| Young Adult (13+) |

"Lemire handles the stuff of a Willa Cather novel with equal poetry, though in images made of lines and spaces rather than words. He renders emotion and temperament in a cartoon face with breathtaking, masterful economy. He manages transitions between present and past and sequences of magic realism as deftly and hauntingly as Ingmar Bergman in Wild Strawberries *and Orson Welles in* Citizen Kane. *Is it too soon to say that Lemire is a major graphic novelist?"*

—Ray Olson, Booklist

"Original, evocative, idiosyncratic and a truly unsparing piece of storytelling... TALES FROM THE FARM, *the folks from Top Shelf note, is 'the first in a trilogy of graphic novels set in a fictionalized version of Lemire's hometown of Essex County, Ontario.' Where do I subscribe? His narrative is unpretentious and unsentimental, and his line is unerring in its ability to find the perfect angle on the ice-coated weather vane, the boot prints on snow, the cigarette dying in an old hockey player's mouth. This is really nice work."*

—Steve Duin, Oregon Live

THE COUNTRY NURSE is the final volume in the critically acclaimed Essex County Trilogy of graphic novels set in a fictionalized version of Lemire's hometown in Ontario, Canada. *THE COUNTRY NURSE* follows a day in the life of Anne Morgan, the peculiar farming community's traveling nurse. As Anne checks in on her favorite patients, the story delves deeper into Essex County's mythology and past, and finally reveals how all three volumes stitch together to quilt a portrait of how loss and regret push and pull at the fabric of family in small town life.

Born in a tiny farming town in Southwestern Ontario, Canada in 1976, cartoonist Jeff Lemire now resides in Toronto. His previous projects include two issues of his self-published anthology comic *Ashtray*, as well as the Xeric Award-winning graphic novel *Lost Dogs*. In 2006, Lemire's work was included as part of the "Comic Craze" exhibit at the Banff Center. An international symposium gathering artists, scholars, curators, publishers, librarians, critics, and writers, "Comic Craze" showcased the best of French and English language Canadian comics and narrative fiction. Jeff's work combines bold, expressive ink work, moody storytelling, and a surprising sense of humanity and sweetness. In addition to the Essex County Trilogy, he is also the writer and illustrator of the sci-fi strip "Fortress" in the quarterly *UR Magazine*.

SULK (VOL 1): BIGHEAD & FRIENDS Jeffery Brown
64-Page Graphic Novel
ISBN 978-1-60309-020-9
$7.00 (US)
Dimensions: 6 1/2" tall x 4 3/4"
Mature (16+)

This pocket-sized, graphic novel series will be a showcase for a variety of Jeffrey Brown's all-new experimental comics. In *SULK (VOL 1): BIGHEAD & FRIENDS*, Bighead returns! And then he dies. And then he returns! It also features all new villains like Beefy Hipster, and introduces Little Bighead — who must stop the villainous Sleeper, before naptime. In *SULK (VOL 2): DEADLY AWESOME*, Jeffrey Brown explores the world of mixed martial arts and the nature of violence in this tribute to no holds barred fighting. In an 80-page fight scene, aging veteran fighter Haruki Rabasaku faces off against young powerhouse Eldark Garprub. With furious striking and technical submission wrestling, this story will entertain readers unfamiliar with the world of cage fighting as well as long time fans of ultimate fighting. Future volumes will contain science fiction and fantasy stories, as well as meditations on the comics form, and more!

After growing up in Michigan, a 25-year-old Jeffrey Brown moved to Chicago in 2000 to pursue an MFA at the School of the Art Institute. By the time he finished his studies, he had abandoned painting and started drawing comics seriously. His first self-published book, *CLUMSY*, appeared seemingly out of nowhere to grab attention from both cartoonists and comics fans. Established as an overly sensitive chronicler of bittersweet adolescent romance and nonsense superhero parody, Brown's current direction remains autobiographical, now examining the minutia of everyday life, the meaning behind our common experiences, and why it's all

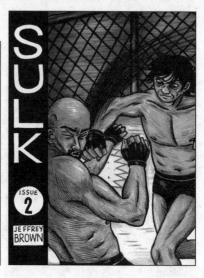

SULK (VOL 2): DEADLY AWESOME Jeffery Brown
96-Page Graphic Novel
ISBN 978-1-60309-031-5
$10.00 (US)
Dimensions: 6 1/2" tall x 4 3/4"
Mature (16+)

kind of funny if you think about it. His work with Top Shelf includes *CLUMSY, UNLIKELY, AEIOU, BE A MAN, I AM GOING TO BE SMALL, MINISULK, EVERY GIRL IS THE END OF THE WORLD FOR ME,* and *FEEBLE ATTEMPTS,* as well as "mainstream" parodies, *INCREDIBLE CHANGE-BOTS* and *BIGHEAD.* He's appeared in a host of anthologies from *McSweeney's* to the *Drawn & Quarterly Showcase,* to Fantagraphics' *Mome* as well as local newspapers such as the *Chicago Reader* and *NewCity.* Jeffrey has been featured on NPR's *This American Life,* in the film documentary *Drawing Between the Lines* by director Bruce Parsons, and even created a short animated music video for the band Death Cab For Cutie.

(Early cover sketch.)

A HIGHLY SKILLED GRAPPLER, RABASAKU QUICKLY AND EASILY PULLS GUARD ON ELDARK.

HE BEGINS LOOKING FOR SUBMISSIONS. WHERE ARE YOU, SUBMISSIONS? ARE YOU HERE? OR HERE? I'M GOING TO FIND YOU..!

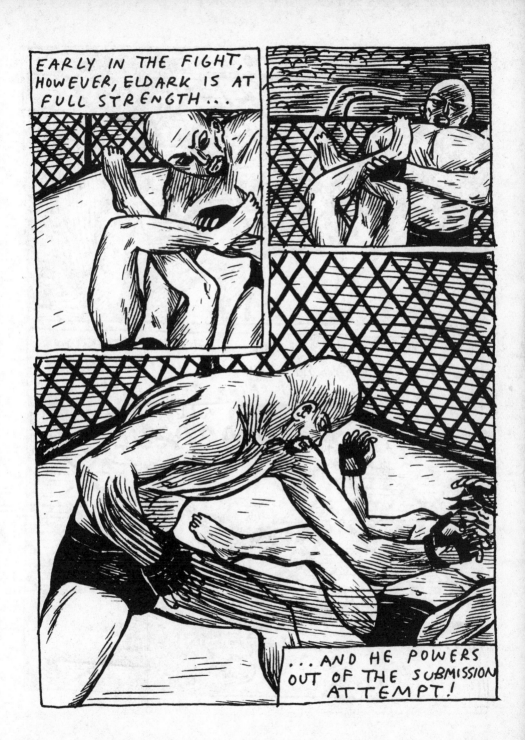

THE TWO FIGHTERS STAND...

SO, HARUKI RABASAKU... YOUR REPUTATION AS A CRAFTY OPPONENT IS JUSTLY EARNED! HOWEVER, YOU WILL FIND THAT CRAFT MAY BE THE ENEMY, WHEN YOU'RE FACING **ELDARK GARPRUB!**

| **DELAYED REPLAYS** |
| Liz Prince |
| 112-Page Graphic Novel |
| ISBN 978-1-60309-012-4 |
| $7.00 (US) |
| Dimensions: 6" x 4 1/4" (landscape) |
| • Mature (16+) |

DELAYED REPLAYS, the second comics collection from Ignatz Award winner Liz Prince (*WILL YOU STILL LOVE ME IF I WET THE BED?*), further explores how one incredibly self-centered twenty-something finds contentment in her everyday life. From the amusing to the banal, Liz's comics are slice-of-life at its best, or if not best, at least most relatable. These strips could easily find their home in many alternative weekly papers, but Liz is too lazy to post them anywhere but her live journal.

Liz Prince has been drawing comics since she was in 3rd grade, and her work has been published since 1994 when she began regularly contributing to the Santa Fe-based zine *Are We There Yet?* From there, the offers didn't stop coming. Her comics have been featured in several zines/comic anthologies, five gallery shows, and she has produced several mini-comics. Influenced by autobiographical greats like Evan Dorkin, Ariel Schrag, James Kochalka, and Jeffrey Brown, her comics mix her real-life foibles with charming cartooning and comic timing. Her fans have described her work as being "cute," making them feel "warm & fuzzy," or simply being "too much information." Liz's first full-length book, *WILL YOU STILL LOVE ME IF I WET THE BED?*, explores the banal and yet somehow fascinating intimacies of her first true love.

The cars are buried

"now there's something you don't see everyday."

a snow mound with a radio antenna!

LIZ PRINCE 2005

kitten self-defense

gee science, you sure are fat.

mew

and farting.

LIZ PRINCE 2005

making a mixtape.

GO OUTSIDE, LIZ! It's a great day!

oh.

Yeah.

LIZ PRINCE 2005

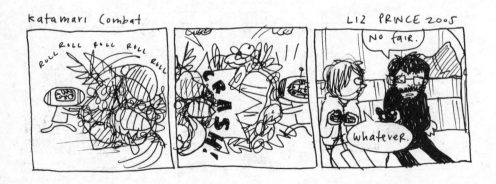

Late night cram session

true ghost stories

bedtime

AMERICAN ELF (BOOK 3)
James Kochalka

192-Page Full-Color Graphic Novel
ISBN 978-1-60309-016-2
$19.95 (US)
Dimensions: 8 1/2" x 8 1/2"
Mature (16+)

Winner of the Ignatz Award for both Outstanding Comic and Outstanding Online Comic.

"Few people keep a diary as consistently and as entertainingly as James Kochalka. [His] tiny strips convey the personalities of him, his family and friends with astounding and impressive ease. Grade: A."
—*Tom McLean,* Variety

Kochalka's diary strip has always been entertaining, but this might be the most action-packed volume of all. His neighbor's car gets firebombed, his little son Eli learns how to invent his own swears (like "pump duck"), and James gets a gun pointed at his face. Most dramatic of all, this volume will introduce a new character, a new little baby Kochalka! Ooohs and aaahs abound. This collection prints all the diary strips from 2006–2007 in gorgeous full-color, including numerous strips that have never appeared online.

TODAY IS THE 20th ANNIVERSARY
OF OUR FIRST KISS
(BUT I GAVE AMY ALL HER PRESENTS YESTERDAY)

JANUARY 1, 2006

WRINKLES

JANUARY 2, 2006

PAJAMA DREAMS

Did you have any dreams last night?

No.

Where'd my dreams go?

Don't worry, I'm sure they'll come back tonight.

In my pajamas!

JANUARY 3, 2006

WESLEY

SOME GIRL WAS ON HER WAY TO BE AN INTERN AT DRAWN & QUARTERLY IN MONTREAL, BUT SHE WAS TURNED AWAY AT THE BORDER. SHE ENDED UP STAYING THE NIGHT AT OUR HOUSE.

What's that girl's name?

Leslie?

Wesley

THE NEXT MORNING

Daddy? Come.

Oh! she woke up

See!

JANUARY 4, 2006

LITTLE PAINTINGS
James Kochalka

48-Page Full-Color Hardcover
ISBN 978-1-60309-017-9
$9.95 (US)
Dimensions: 5 1/2" x 7 1/2"
Mature (16+)

This delightful and deliriously colorful artbook contains several hundred of Kochalka's best "little paintings" from the last decade. Kochalka began making little paintings as something to sell to fans at conventions, but they quickly became a consuming obsession that led to several incredibly successful gallery shows at Giant Robot. Dozens and dozens of cute kitties and fuzzy creatures dominate the book, but as with all Kochalka's work, a deeper theme flows through the undercurrents ... in this case it's contemporary America's emotional plight following the harrowing events of 9/11. Ultimately, *LITTLE PAINTINGS* is a celebration of the triumph of imagination over the harsh realities of the physical world. Very beautiful.

| LITTLE PAINTINGS

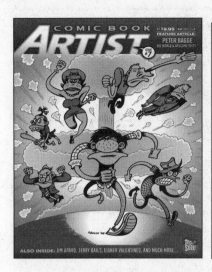

COMIC BOOK ARTIST (VOL 2) #7: THE PETER BAGGE ISSUE

Edited by Jon B. Cooke

136-Page Perfect-Bound Magazine (with a 16-page full-color section)
ISBN 978-1-60309-021-6
$9.95 (US)
Dimensions: 8 1/2" x 11"
Young Adult (13+)

COMIC BOOK ARTIST returns (promise!!) with a blast of Bagge as we celebrate the captivating life and hilarious work of renowned cartoonist Peter Bagge (of *Hate* and *Neat Stuff* fame), with a career-spanning interview and eye-popping collection of rarely seen and unpublished art. This comprehensive feature covers it all: Peter's dysfunctional (and typically all-American) suburban middle-class upbringing; his time in New York City as *Punk* magazine cartoonist; the Seattle days of struggle while producing *Neat Stuff*; the *Hate*-filled success of his most celebrated creations, Buddy Bradley and Co.; and his current work on *Apocalypse Nerd*. Also in this issue: *Weirdo* magazine gets the *CBA* treatment, with exclusive interviews with cartoonist genius Robert Crumb (who created the legendary 1980s/90s humor rag), the aforementioned Mr. Bagge (Crumb's editorial successor), and Aline Kominsky-Crumb (Crumb's spouse and editor of *Weirdo's* final run). Also included is a tribute to the late, great historian, Dr. Jerry Bails, the father of comics fandom. Plus a delightful gallery of the great Will Eisner's handmade Valentines drawn for his wife, the debut of a slew of new columnists, and the return of our regular contributors, all showcased in the magazine's newly expanded format. Buddy, this is one *CBA* you can't afford to miss!

COMIC BOOK ARTIST (VOL 2) #8: THE TONY HARRIS ISSUE
Edited by Jon B. Cooke

136-Page Perfect-Bound Magazine (with a 16-page full-color section)
ISBN 978-1-60309-022-3
$9.95 (US)
Dimensions: 8 1/2" x 11"
Young Adult (13+)

In this issue, *COMIC BOOK ARTIST* headlines the dynamic visions of the artist and co-originator of *Starman* and *Ex Machina*, the terrific Tony Harris. Complete with a huge interview — from his military "brat" childhood; to his groundbreaking emergence nearly 20 years ago as a talent to watch; to collaborations on the celebrated *Starman* with writer James Robinson, and his current creative partnership with superstar scribe Brian K. Vaughn on the hit series *Ex Machina* — not to mention a startling art gallery of Harris masterworks. Our "CBA Classic" section focuses on the life and career of the late artist Jim Aparo, complete with interview, art gallery and essays. Plus we spotlight another "tony" delineator, Mr. Tony Tallarico, whose original stylings have graced the pages of American comic books since the 1960s. There's also a T. Motley sketchbook, our crew of cantankerous columnists, and the usual array of *CBA* goodies to absorb. Reach for the stars with this stellar issue of *CBA!*

Jon B. Cooke, editor of the multiple Eisner Award-winning magazine *COMIC BOOK ARTIST*, was born a full-fledged comic book geek. He started collecting funny books in the early 70s, inspired by the artistry of Jack Kirby and the King's *Fourth World* titles. For a time during those formative years, Cooke edited the fledgling fan effort *Omegazine*, which reached a whopping circulation of 25 or so, a fanzine his three brothers contributed to. Cooke attended the University of Rhode Island in the early 1980s as a history/journalism major, where he developed a taste for print work as editor of the campus hippie/lefty magazine, the *Great Swamp Gazette*. In 1995, Cooke began contributing to *The Jack Kirby Collector* published by TwoMorrows, and by 1998 he created *COMIC BOOK ARTIST*, producing 25 issues for the company. During that time he also edited *The Warren Companion*, *Streetwise*, and two *CBA* collections, as well as designed numerous books on comics-related subjects, including *The Amazing World of Carmine Infantino*, *Kimota! The Miracleman Companion*, *The Art of Nick Cardy*, and issues of *Alter Ego*. Once, in the Dark Ages, Cooke was a graphic designer and art director for East Coast advertising agencies, but now he lives a dream job helming *CBA*, the magazine devoted to the love of comics old and new. He resides in Rhode Island with his wife, Beth, and three sons, Ben, Josh and Danny. With immense pride and enthusiasm, the editor moved *CBA* to Top Shelf Productions in 2003, where it has remained since.

FUTURE RELEASES

Here are the details on a few of the titles Top Shelf has planned for
2009 and 2010 — just to whet your appetite!

MARSHAL LAW (OMNIBUS). Pat Mills & Kevin O'Neill
THE LEAGUE OF EXTRAORDINARY GENTLEMEN (VOL III): CENTURY.
Alan Moore & Kevin O'Neill
THE MOON & SERPENT BUMPER BOOK OF MAGIC.
Alan Moore, Steve Moore, and various artists.
KISSYPOO GARDEN. Craig Thompson
ALEC (LIFE-SIZE OMNIBUS). Eddie Campbell
BACCHUS (TWO-VOLUME OMNIBUS). Eddie Campbell
THE SURROGATES 2.0: FLESH & BONE. Robert Venditti & Brett Weldele
THE HOMELAND DIRECTIVE. Robert Venditti & Kristian Donaldson
DOGS DAY END. Brian Wood & Nikki Cook
JUNCTION TRUE. Ray Fawkes & Vince Locke
INFINITE KUNG-FU. Kagan McLeod
BB WOLF & THE 3 LP'S. J.D. Arnold & Rich Koslowski
HEY, MISTER: COME HELL OR HIGHWATER PANTS.
Pete Sickman-Garner

MARSHAL LAW (OMNIBUS)

Pat Mills & Kevin O'Neill

A 2009 Release

500+ Page Full-Color Graphic Novel

ISBN 978-1-60309-023-0

Dimensions: 7 1/4" x 11"

Mature (16+)

Marshal Law CGI Art by Nick Percival.

BEHIND THE MASK — Secrets. Secret identities. Secret lusts. Secret hates. The dark and sordid world of Super Heroes...

Pull down the trunks, you won't like what you see.

When Superman goes rogue, you call on the Court of Last Resort ... MARSHAL LAW!

The government has commissioned living weapons of mass destruction to wage war on terror. The survivors return home broken, bitter, insane. Some form gangs, some go psycho. Some turn into 'A' list celebrities with 'A' bomb fists. The city is now a war zone.

San Futuro needs a Super Cop to enforce summary justice. His eyes will reflect the rocket's red glare. He is Twilight's Last Gleaming... MARSHAL LAW !

A bad choice is better than no choice at all.

Top Shelf is proud to announce that it has signed Pat Mills and Kevin O'Neill's MARSHAL LAW, and will publish *MARSHAL LAW OMNIBUS* next year — *the* all-up, one-volume, full-color, 600(+)-page definitive MARSHAL LAW collection.

Chris Staros and Brett Warnock have been huge fans of the series since the beginning, and are elated to be able to put out this super-deluxe collection of the entire series.

The anti-heroes' anti-hero will never look better.

Pat Mills is the British comics writer best known as the co-creator of *Marshal Law* (with artist Kevin O'Neill), and the creator of the science-fiction themed British magazine, *2000AD*. His strips for this include *Nemesis the Warlock* (also with Kevin O'Neill), *Judge Dredd*, *Sláine*, *Greysuit*, and *Defoe: 1666*. He is currently writing Book 8 of the best-selling French graphic novel series *Requiem, Vampire Knight* with art by Olivier Ledroit, Book 4 of *Claudia, Vampire Knight*, with art by Frank Tacito (both reprinted in *Heavy Metal*), various other French series, and a *Doctor Who* radio play.

Born in London in 1953, Kevin O'Neill is the British comics illustrator best known as the co-creator of *The League of Extraordinary Gentlemen* (with Alan Moore), *Marshal Law* (with writer Pat Mills), and *Nemesis the Warlock* for *2000AD* (also with Pat Mills). With one of the most unique and detailed styles in comics, he has deservedly earned an enormous worldwide fanbase. Top Shelf is honored to be working with Kevin on *The League of Extraordinary Gentlemen (Volume III)*, due to begin publication in 2009.

Marshal Law CGI Art by Nick Percival.

THE LEAGUE OF EXTRAORDINARY GENTLEMAN (VOL III) CENTURY

Alan Moore & Kevin O'Neill

A 2009 Release

#1 (of 3) ISBN 978-1-60309-000-1
#2 (of 3) ISBN 978-1-60309-006-3
#3 (of 3) ISBN 978-1-60309-007-0

Dimensions: 6 1/2" x 10"

Mature (16+)

Beginning In 2009…

The third volume detailing the exploits of Miss Wilhelmina Murray and her extraordinary colleagues, *CENTURY*, is a 216-page epic spanning almost a hundred years. Divided into three 72-page chapters — each a self-contained narrative to avoid frustrating cliffhanger delays between episodes — this monumental tale takes place in three distinct eras, building to an apocalyptic conclusion occurring in our own current twenty-first century.

Chapter one is set against a backdrop of London, 1910, twelve years after the failed Martian invasion and nine years since England put a man upon the moon. With Halley's Comet passing overhead, the nation prepares for the coronation of King George V, and far away on his South Atlantic Island, the science-pirate Captain Nemo is dying. In the bowels of the British Museum, Carnacki the ghost-finder is plagued by visions of a shadowy occult order who are attempting to create something called a Moonchild, while on London's dockside the most notorious serial murderer of the previous century has returned to carry on his grisly trade. Working for Mycroft Holmes' British Intelligence alongside a rejuvenated Allan Quartermain, the reformed thief Anthony Raffles, and the eternal warrior Orlando, Miss Murray is drawn into a brutal opera acted out upon the waterfront by players that include the furiously angry Pirate Jenny and the charismatic butcher known as Mac the Knife.

Chapter two takes place almost sixty years later in the psychedelic daze of Swinging London during 1968, a place where Tadukic Acid Diethylamide 26 is the drug of choice, and where different underworlds are starting to overlap dangerously to an accompaniment of sit-ins and sitars. The vicious gangster bosses of London's East End find themselves brought into contact with a counter-culture underground of mystical and medicated flowerchildren, or amoral pop-stars on the edge of psychological disintegration and developing a taste for Satanism. Alerted to a threat concerning the same magic order that she and her colleagues were investigating during 1910, a thoroughly modern Mina Murray and her dwindling league of comrades attempt to navigate the perilous rapids of London's hippy and criminal subculture, as well as the twilight world of its occultists. Starting to buckle from the pressures of the twentieth century and the weight of

their own endless lives, Mina and her companions must nevertheless prevent the making of a Moonchild that might well turn out to be the antichrist.

In chapter three, the narrative draws to its cataclysmic close in London 2008. The magical child whose ominous coming has been foretold for the past hundred years has now been born and has grown up to claim his dreadful heritage. His promised aeon of unending terror can commence, the world can now be ended starting with North London, and there is no League, extraordinary or otherwise, that now stands in his way. The bitter, intractable war of attrition in Q'umar crawls bloodily to its fifth year, away in Kashmir a Sikh terrorist with a now-nuclear-armed submarine wages a holy war against Islam that might push the whole world into atomic holocaust, and in a London mental institution there's a patient who insists that she has all the answers.

Drawing from the fiction, theatre, film, and television culture of the twentieth century as artfully as the preceding volumes drew upon the literature of the nineteenth, this first installment of the League's adventures to be co-published by Top Shelf Productions and Knockabout takes our familiar cast of characters ... plus several previously unfamiliar ... and propels them into a new age, a new world every bit as strange and savage as the colourful Victorian era they were born to. More than this, with its third volume the League's exploits move into a different realm of format, artistry, and story-telling as this remarkable series sets out to explore the full limits of the vast fictional cosmos that it has marked as its territory. A unified field theory of fiction as much as a comic-book story, *The League of Extraordinary Gentlemen (Vol III): Century* is sure to be like nothing you have ever read, and will be co-published in three lavish, full-color individual volumes commencing in 2009.

Praise for the first volume of *LEAGUE OF EXTRAORDINARY GENTLEMEN*:

"A stunning coup de grace is delivered with this masterful pairing of Victorian adventure fiction's greatest characters and the old war-horse of the super-group. With the stunning The League of Extraordinary Gentlemen, *it would be no exaggeration to say that Alan Moore has produced a near-perfect piece of adventure fiction that is clever, literate, rich with excitement and hard to put down.*

"With no shortage of action, Moore and O' Neill sustain a high level of suspense, intrigue, mystery and terrific wit that all contribute to an indispensable read. O'Neill's art, so memorable in Marshal Law, *produces a London filled with vivid, magnificent architecture and a malevolent atmosphere ripe with thrills and danger. An unmitigated triumph —pure and simple."*

—Danny Graydon, Amazon

Alan Moore is widely regarded as the best and most influential writer in the history of comics. His seminal works include *LOST GIRLS*, *Miracleman* and *Watchmen*, for which he won the coveted Hugo Award. Never one to limit himself in form or content, Moore has also published a novel, *VOICE OF THE FIRE*, an epic poem, *THE MIRROR OF LOVE*, and three of his ground-breaking graphic novels, *FROM HELL*, *V for Vendetta*, and *THE LEAGUE OF EXTRAORDINARY GENTLEMEN*, have been adapted to the silver screen. Moore currently resides in Northampton, England, where he's simultaneously working on his next novel, *Jerusalem*, as well as two graphic novels: *THE LEAGUE OF EXTRAORDINARY GENTLEMEN (Vol III): CENTURY* with Kevin O'Neill, and *THE MOON & SERPENT BUMPER BOOK OF MAGIC* with Steve Moore.

THE MOON & SERPENT BUMPER BOOK OF MAGIC

Alan Moore, Steve Moore,
and various artists

A 2010 Release
A 320-Page Super-Deluxe Hardcover
ISBN 978-1-60309-001-8
Young Adult (13+)

Splendid news for boys and girls, and guaranteed salvation for humanity! Messrs. Steve and Alan Moore, current proprietors of the celebrated Moon & Serpent Grand Egyptian Theatre of Marvels (sorcery by appointment since circa 150 AD) are presently engaged in producing a clear and practical grimoire of the occult sciences that offers endless necromantic fun for all the family. Exquisitely illuminated by a host of adepts including Kevin O'Neill, Melinda Gebbie, John Coulthart, Steve Parkhouse, José Villarrubia and other stellar talents (to be named shortly), this marvelous and unprecedented tome promises to provide all that the reader could conceivably need in order to commence a fulfilling new career as a diabolist.

Its contents include profusely illustrated instructional essays upon this ancient sect's theories of magic, notably the key dissertation "Adventures in Thinking" which gives reliable advice as to how entry into the world of magic may be readily achieved. Further to this, a number of "Rainy Day" activity pages present lively and entertaining things-to-do once the magical state has been attained, including such popular pastimes as divination, etheric travel, and the conjuring of a colourful multitude of sprits, deities, dead people, and infernal entities from the pit, all of whom are sure to become your new best friends.

Also contained within this extravagant compendium of thaumaturgic lore is a history of magic from the last ice-age to the present day, told in a series of easy-to-absorb pictorial biographies of fifty great enchanters and complemented by a variety of picture stories depicting events ranging from the Paleolithic origins of art, magic, language, and consciousness to the rib-tickling comedy exploits of Moon & Serpent founder Alexander the False Prophet ("He's fun, he's fake, he's got a talking snake!").

In addition to these manifold delights, the adventurous reader will also discover a series of helpful travel guides to mind-wrenching alien dimensions that are within comfortable walking distance, as well as profiles of the many quaint local inhabitants that one might bump into at these exotic resorts. A full range of entertainments will be provided, encompassing such diverse novelties and pursuits as a lavishly decorated decadent pulp tale of occult adventure recounted in the serial form, a full set of this sinister and deathless cult's never-before-seen Tarot cards, a fold-out Kabalistic board game in which the first player to achieve enlightenment wins providing he or she doesn't make a big deal about it, and even a pop-up Theatre of Marvels that serves as both a Renaissance memory theatre and a handy portable shrine for today's multi-tasking magician on the move.

Completing this almost unimaginable treasure-trove are a matching pair of lengthy theses revealing the ultimate meaning of both the Moon and the Serpent in a manner that makes transparent the much obscured secret of magic, happiness, sex, creativity, and the known Universe, while at the same time explaining why these lunar and ophidian symbols feature so prominently in the order's peculiar name. (Manufacturer's disclaimer: this edition does not, however, reveal why the titular cabal of magicians consider themselves to be either grand or Egyptian. Let the buyer beware.)

A colossal and audacious publishing triumph of three hundred and twenty pages, beautifully produced in the finest tradition of educational literature for young people, *The Moon & Serpent Bumper Book of Magic* will transform your lives, your reality, and any spare lead that you happen to have laying around into the purest and most radiant gold.

Often described as the man who led Alan Moore astray (usually by Alan himself), Steve Moore is a cranky old hermit who hardly lives in the 21st century at all. Since starting in comics forty years ago, he's written mainly science fiction and fantasy strips (sometimes under the name Pedro Henry) for a variety of British and American publishers, including titles such as *Jonni Future*, *Laser-Eraser & Pressbutton*, and *Tales of Telguuth*. Occasionally taking a break to work on non-fiction in the oriental, historical and Fortean fields, he's written on the *I Ching* (*The Trigrams of Han*) and edited the scholarly journal *Fortean Studies*. 2006 saw his novelization of the movie *V for Vendetta*, and he's currently putting the finishing touches to an original novel, *Somnium*. A Fellow of the Royal Asiatic Society, he lives in London, and is neither related to Alan Moore nor anywhere near as hairy...

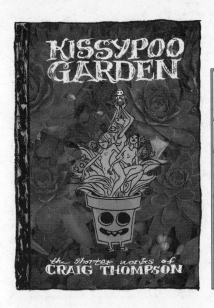

KISSYPOO GARDEN
Craig Thompson

A 2009 Release

Graphic Novel Collection with Black & White and Full-Color Sections

ISBN 978-1-891830-82-2

Dimensions: 6 1/2" x 9"

Mature (16+)

Slated for the 2009 timeframe, *KISSYPOO GARDEN* will be a 200(+)-page collection of Craig Thompson's short stories and "comics poems." Combining out-of-print minicomics and stories published in obscure anthologies, along with never-before-published pieces, sketchbook excerpts, and a full-color section compiling the best of his *Nickelodeon Magazine* strips, this gorgeous tome will be a sure-fire hit with comics fans everywhere. And for those of you who were never able to get copies of Craig's minis *DOOT DOOT GARDEN* or *BIBLE DOODLES*, these will also be reprinted, along with approximately 50 pages of brand new material.

"*Kissypoo Garden* is the title of a mini-comic I began and left unfinished in 1997," says Craig Thompson. "I had a bad habit back then of getting ten pages into something and then abandoning it. My intent is to see this story to completion some ten years later, and hopefully gain some insight about carrying through with a creative vision."
—Craig Thompson

Craig Thompson was born in Traverse City, Michigan in 1975 and raised outside a small town in central Wisconsin. His award-winning graphic novels at Top Shelf include *BLANKETS* and *CARNET DE VOYAGE*.

ALEC (LIFE-SIZE OMNIBUS)
Eddie Campbell

A 2009 Release

640-Page Graphic Novel

ISBN 978-1-60309-025-4

Mature (16+)

"Alec is magic, and even if I knew how all of it was done I'd be doing you a disservice if I pointed out the wires and mirrors. [...] It is written by someone who obviously finds being alive an endless source of novelty and conundrum."

—Alan Moore

While some might only know Eddie Campbell through his collaboration with Alan Moore on *FROM HELL*, Eddie has published (or been a part of) an impressive 200 comic books and graphic novels to date; with most of that work centering around his two great continuities: *ALEC* (a.k.a. Alec MacGarry) and *BACCHUS* (a.k.a. Deadface).

If this surprises you, it's probably due to the unserialized nature of many of his releases — something that's about to be cured with the Omnibus collections of both *ALEC* and *BACCHUS*…

ALEC is a brilliant and insightful romp through Eddie's life, and it represents one of the best — and first! — works in the autobiographical-comics genre. In it, we witness Eddie's progression from "beer to wine," or to put it more accurately, his inevitable maturation through time. Whether it's tales of his early pub-crawlin' days, or glimpses into his current private life with "wifey" and kids, there are "truths" here that transcend the factual and paint a picture of the way life should be.

The *ALEC (LIFE-SIZE OMNIBUS)* will collect all the stories from *THE KING CANUTE CROWD, THREE PIECE SUIT, HOW TO BE AN ARTIST, AFTER THE SNOOTER*, as well as the very early out-of-print *ALEC* stories and tons of bonus, never-before-seen material. It will definitely be the definitive *ALEC* tome.

A tale of
horror
by
Eddie
Campbell
Feb '95

The Snooter buffers in on a humid night.

I am cleaning my empty bottle collection...

...like they were doing in the galley of the *Marie Celeste*

...on that dark and doleful day.

They too saw the sign.

I too fail to take heed...

...and feel only sympathy for the creature.

The Snooter has lodged himself down behind my archives.

I bring him to safety.

How did a thing so strange get to live to be so big...

...in this, the age of the small poppy?

I watch the Snooter depart, nevermore to see his nasal tendril...

...except for the next time, which is in Yocky's mouth.

The rash is not preceeded by any prediction...

"Leo: Mark time businesswise. Health average."

And it had this long tendril coming from its snout.

Are you sure you hadn't been drinking?

... or so wifey says. I don't follow the horoscopes.

My fingers look like porridge from days of auld lang syne.

I have not been sleeping well for years.

In the dark silence of night, all horrors are unwrapped.

Must warn the world.

THE TOPSHELF BOYS

We also have stickers, coasters, matchboxes and posters to help enhance Topshelf's presence in your store.

Eddie Campbell 8. '00.

I have to catch the next plane out. I don't think Nita's dad will see out the day.

Aw, we're all on a bus to shitsville, man.

So you're going to have to sell this to the retailers.

Hey, no sweat.

Now the list contains only our BEST SELLING GRAPHIC NOVELS, with a total retail value of FIVE... HUNDRED... DOLLARS. THEY only have to pay ONE NINE NINE

Cool

That's 60% off. SIXTY. PER. CENT.

Discount city, man.

We're even going to ship the books at our OWN expense

Awesome

They don't even have to pay for THIRTY DAYS! We'll invoice them.

Wow

And not only that, but anything they can't sell after thirty days, we'll replace with anything else from the list of an equivalent value.

Have you got all that? Play it back to me.

Okay

Hey, dude! Here's the spiel on the deal...

BACCHUS (TWO-VOLUME OMNIBUS)

Eddie Campbell

A 2010 Release
Two 560-Page Graphic Novels
ISBN 978-1-60309-026-1 (Vol 1)
ISBN 978-1-60309-027-8 (Vol 2)
Mature (16+)

"BACCHUS *mixes air hijacks and ancient gods, gangland drama and legends, police procedural and mythic fantasy, swimming pool cleaners and classics. It shouldn't work, of course, and it works like a charm. ... Eddie Campbell is the unsung King of comic books. ... The man's a genius, and that's an end to it.*"

—*Neil Gaiman*

"*Though one often gets in trouble when saying things like this, I'd like to go on record as stating the following: 'BACCHUS is the ultimate comic book!' Why? Because, by some creative miracle, it possesses every possible quality one could hope for: a unique and engaging art style; a brilliantly crafted and intriguing story; completely believable and captivating characters; an undercurrent of humor, sarcasm, and irony; a thought-provoking subtext full of social and political realism; a well-researched examination of history; and, yes — I'll admit it! — superheroes. In its own weird way,* BACCHUS *is actually a revisionist-superhero tale told in epic Greek proportions.*"

—*Chris Staros,* The Staros Report (1996)

BACCHUS is a wild and hilarious mythological adventure imbued with unparalleled social and political insight. It's a story of a few Greek gods who have somehow managed to survive the last four millennia. And even though they're the "wisest" and most powerful beings on Earth, they can't seem to rise above the whirlwind of petty grudges and skirmishes that bind them.

The *BACCHUS (2-VOLUME OMNIBUS)* will collect all 1,000 pages of the *BACCHUS* saga — yes, that's ONE THOUSAND PAGES!! — the entire epic in two giant 500-page volumes. It's time that this long out-of-print masterpiece be introduced to an entirely new comics generation.

‹ DON SKYLLA. HERE'S THE GUY YOU WANTED. ›

‹ HEY, THIS IS *BACCHUS, THE GOD OF WINE.* TREAT HIM WITH SOME RESPECT. ›

COME IN, BACCHUS. EXCUSE THE FORMALITY. IT'S THE *DAY OF THE DEAD.* ONCE A YEAR I COME DOWN HERE TO THE *CATACOMBE DEI CAPPUCCINI* TO DINE WITH MY ANCESTORS AND DISCUSS FAMILY *BUSINESS.*

WHAT HAS THAT TO DO WITH ME?

I AM FACING A RATHER DIFFICULT SITUATION, BACCHUS: POSSIBLY AN ALL-OUT WAR.

AND AS IN THE *TROJAN WAR,* THE GODS ARE BEING SOLICITED FOR THEIR PATRONAGE...

...BEING ASKED TO TAKE SIDES, IN OTHER WORDS.

I'M NO GOOD IN A SCRAP. I'M NOT THAT SORT OF A GOD.

AND IT PROBABLY WON'T BE THAT SORT OF A WAR.

BUT THESE ARE DISMAL TIMES. ONE DOES NOT HAVE A LOT OF CHOICES. YOU, BACCHUS, ARE THE LAST SURVIVING *FERTILITY GOD* ON OUR PLANET.

I MEAN, NOW IT CAN'T BE A COINCIDENCE THAT THE DAY *YOU* ARRIVE IN SICILY, *ETNA* GIVES US ITS BIGGEST ERUPTION SINCE *1971.*

APART FROM THAT, I HAPPEN TO BE THE PRESENT TRUSTEE OF AN OLD TALISMAN OF YOURS.

I had a hunch it might turn up very soon.

Earth, Water, Air, Fire - part 2 - page 11

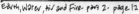

Earth, Water, Air and Fire - part 2- page 12

HEY, YOU! YOU GOTTA WEAR THE BLACK TIE.

I'LL SORT IT OUT.

DON SKYLLA, THOSE GUYS STOP AT NOTHING.

WE GOTTA BRING THE WAR TO THEM BEFORE THEY BRING IT HERE.

BUT WE DON'T WANNA MAKE NO RASH MOVES, HORSE-DOCTOR.

AH! OUR GUEST OF HONOUR ARRIVES!

MY FRIENDS, THIS IS BACCHUS, THE GOD OF WINE, OUR DIVINE PATRON IN THE BUSINESS THAT LIES AHEAD OF US.

LOAD YOUR GLASSES RESPECTFULLY!

Earth, Water, Air and Fire - part 2 - page 15

WHAT EXACTLY DO YOUR PRAYERS ASK OF ME, SKYLLA?

TO WEAR A .44-CALIBRE SUIT AND GO VISIT SOME GUY?

AW, NO, BACCHUS. WE GOT ALL KINDA HALFWITS WHO CAN DO THAT. YOU JUST LET YOUR AURA FILL UP OUR LITTLE GATHERING HERE.

THIS ALL SOUNDS A BIT TOO MYSTICAL FOR A COSA NOSTRA BANQUET.

HEY!-YOU TAKING PIKCHAS OF ME?!

I'll sort it out.

GIMME THAT CAMRA!

THE WAR HAS STARTED.

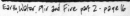

THE SURROGATES 2.0: FLESH & BONE

Robert Venditti & Brett Weldele

A 2009 Release
A Full-Color Graphic Novel
ISBN 978-1-60309-018-6
Dimensions: 6 5/8" x 10 1/8"
Young Adult (13+)

Praise for *THE SURROGATES 1.0*:

"Good science fiction is hard to come by, but Venditti's blend of technology, crime drama and social commentary makes for the most original sci-fi mythology in years."

—Wizard Magazine

"An absolutely fascinating piece of work — heartfelt and thoughtful."

—Fantasy & Science Fiction

In a dark downtown alley in Central Georgia Metropolis, a juvenile prank goes too far and a homeless man is killed. When the ensuing investigation reveals that the attackers aren't who they appeared to be, justice depends on the testimony of a single eyewitness — a street snitch with a history of providing information to a uniformed cop named Harvey Greer. Harvey is placed on special assignment to track down the informant, but others have their own designs, including a wealthy socialite and an ex-con turned religious leader known to his followers as The Prophet. As days pass and anger among the anti-surrogate population grows, the city stands on a razor's edge. Will punishment be exacted in a courtroom or on the streets?

Set fifteen years prior to the events of the first volume, *FLESH AND BONE* sheds light on the past that binds the cast together. From the streets of Central Georgia Metropolis to the boardroom of Virtual Self, Inc., it takes us on a journey through a city struggling to come to grips with its present. As much a cautionary tale as a story of suspense, this book reminds us that tomorrow will be determined by the choices we make today.

Robert Venditti broke into comics the old-fashioned way — by starting out in the mailroom. He began working for Top Shelf in 2002, and a few months later pitched the idea for his first graphic novel, *THE SURROGATES*. The rest, as they say, "is history," as *THE SURROGATES* is soon to be released as a major motion picture. Venditti lives in the Atlanta area where he continues to write comics and work full-time for Top Shelf.

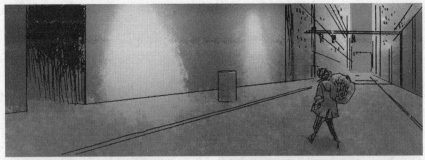

SPARE ME A DOLLAR, SIR?

A *DOLLAR?* IT'LL COST A LOT MORE THAN *THAT* TO FIX WHAT'S WRONG WITH YOU.

SERIOUSLY, LOOK AT THESE CLOTHES. I DIDN'T THINK *ANYTHING* COULD LOOK AS BAD AS YOU *STINK*, BUT YOU MANAGED TO PULL IT OFF.

WHAT'S THAT?

HEY, *I* KNOW WHAT HE NEEDS.

A *BEATING.* YOU KNOW, LIKE THE *MAID* DOES WITH THE RUGS.

YEAH, THAT'S NOT A BAD IDEA . . .

WHAT DO YOU SAY? YOU WANT US TO HELP YOU SHAKE THE DIRT OUT?

GROSS! IT SMELLS LIKE *PISS!*

I DON'T WANT NO TROUBLE.

SHOULD'VE THOUGHT ABOUT THAT BEFORE YOU CHUCKED A BOTTLE AT US.

YEAH, WE WERE JUST HAVING A *LITTLE FUN* WITH YOU BEFORE--

--BUT NOW WE'RE GOING TO HAVE *A LOT.*

DUDE, YOUR DAD'S GOING TO *FREAK.*

YOU SHOULDN'T HAVE DONE THAT, *BONER.*

NOW IT'S OUR TURN TO SEE WHAT *YOU'VE* GOT UNDERNEATH.

HOW MANY *LICKS* DO YOU THINK IT'LL TAKE TO GET TO THE CENTER?

HA HA HA HA

"SON, WHY AREN'T YOU IN BED?"

THE HOMELAND DIRECTIVE
Robert Venditti & Kristian Donaldson

A 2010 Release

A Full-Color Graphic Novel

ISBN 978-1-60309-024-7

Dimensions: 6 5/8" x 10 1/8"

Young Adult (13+)

As head of the National Center for Infectious Diseases, Dr. Laura Regan is one of the world's foremost authorities on viral and bacteriological study. Having dedicated her career to halting the spread of infectious disease, she has always considered herself one of the good guys. But when her research partner is murdered and Laura is blamed for the crime, she finds herself at the heart of a vast and deadly conspiracy. Aided by three rogue federal agents who believe the government is behind the frame-up, Laura must evade law enforcement, mercenaries, and a team of cyber-detectives who know more about her life than she does—all while trying to expose a sinister plot that will impact the lives of every American.

Set in the Orwellian present, *THE HOMELAND DIRECTIVE* is a modern-day political/medical thriller about a faction within the US government that conspires to expand the surveillance state. Part Tom Clancy, part Michael Crichton, and all high-octane suspense, *THE HOMELAND DIRECTIVE* confronts one of the vital questions of our time: In an era when technology can either doom or save us, is it possible for personal privacy and national security to coexist?

Dallas based artist, Kristian Donaldson, has been working in comics since 2004, having done work for DC/Vertigo Comics, Marvel Comics, IDW Publishing, Image Comics, White Wolf Games, Boom!Studios, Klasky Csupo Animation, and world renowned architect Philippe Starck. He attended art school, where he earned 8 degrees, in such varied fields as "Advanced Quantam Cartooning" and "Nuclear Photoshopping." His grandmother would describe him to any young ladies in earshot as "a keeper." He may or may not be the kind of jerk who writes about himself in the third person.

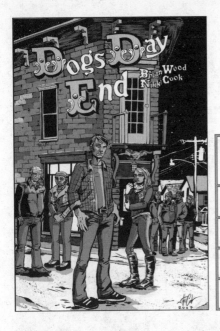

| **DOGS DAY END** |
| Brian Wood & Nikki Cook |
| A 2009 Release |
| Graphic Novel |
| ISBN 978-1-891830-59-4 |
| Mature (16+) |

Following up on the time-honored adage "you can't go home again," *DOGS DAY END* details the personal journey of 30-year-old Andrew Maguire, pulled back to the small upstate hometown of his childhood by his mother as she enters the final stages of cancer. Once back, he revisits the demons of his youth: his estranged father, resentful ex-buddies, and his jilted high school sweetheart. As the twin pressures of the past and the present threaten to bury him, Andrew makes an all-or-nothing decision to come to terms with it all. *DOGS DAY END* reads like an indy film on paper, reminiscent of Eternal Sunshine of the Spotless Mind and Garden State, but with the edge of Closer and Affliction.

Brian Wood released his first series, *Channel Zero*, in 1997 to considerable critical acclaim and has continued to produce comics and graphic novels at a brisk pace ever since, becoming one of the most important indy creators of the last decade. Standout works include his *Couriers* and *Channel Zero* series, *Demo*, *Local*, *Supermarket*, *DMZ*, and fourteen cover illustrations for Warren Ellis' Global Frequency. He has earned multiple Eisner Award nominations, and is currently under an exclusive contract for DC/Vertigo, where Wood continues to write his unique brand of eclectic creator-owned work.

Nikki Cook grew up in a Minnesotan town you'd need a magnifying glass to find on a map. There she spent her time pounding on her brothers and reading through huge piles of comic books. This apparently had an effect on her, because after art school in Minneapolis, she scuttled off to New York City to bury herself in ink. In New York, you can find her working tirelessly on *DOGS DAY END* with Brian Wood.

JUNCTION TRUE
Ray Fawkes & Vince Locke

A 2009 Release

128-Page Full-Color Graphic Novel

ISBN 978-1-891830-99-0

Mature (16+)

"It's the freaks who always change the world..."

"...We brought down the genome patents and open-sourced the medical profession. That was us. We crashed the plastic surgery business. We paved the way for parasite chic. The body became a new kind of playground and we, celebrating the future, we became the Neumod."

In the near-future Neumod culture of parasite addicts and hardcore one-upmanship, Dirk Brody has found love. He'll do anything to prove himself to the woman of his dreams – even if it means blurring the boundaries of his flesh with the radical, illegal Junction True procedure. Once he starts, he can never go back...

Ray Fawkes has been writing professionally since 2001. His comic book works include the critically acclaimed *Spookshow*, *The Apocalipstix* with Cameron Stewart; and *Mnemovore*, a horror title for DC/Vertigo with Hans Rodionoff and Mike Huddleston. His intense, dark style has garnered acclaim from comic fans and professional contemporaries alike. Reviews have declared his work to be "distinctive...intelligent and sharply written" (*PopImage*), and "haunting, intriguing, with a hint of noir" (*Cold Cut* Spotlight Review). Ray is based in Toronto, Canada.

Vince Locke is an accomplished artist who began work in 1986 illustrating *Deadworld*, a zombie horror comic that soon became an underground hit. Since then, his illustrative talents in comics have included *The Sandman*, *Batman*, *The Spectre*, and *A History of Violence*, which was later made into a movie directed by David Cronenberg and starring Viggo Mortensen. Locke has also gained notoriety by creating ultra-violent watercolor paintings used as album covers for the death metal band Cannibal Corpse. He lives with his wife and son in Michigan, where he continues to draw and paint many things.

| **INFINITE KUNG-FU** |
| Kagan McLeod |
| A 2009 Release |
| Graphic Novel |
| ISBN 978-1-891830-83-9 |
| Young Adult (13+) |

INFINITE KUNG-FU walks you through familiar corridors in the house of martial mayhem, but still smashes you through walls of wonder and into rooms where kung fu is afraid to go. The Martial World is ruled by a mysterious emperor whose five armies are each headed by a cruel and highly skilled kung fu master. Lei Kung, a soldier in one of these armies, grows tired of his master's evil ways and seeks enlightenment elsewhere. However, he soon finds that he's been chosen as the one who will put an end to the emperor's tyrannical rule, personally. Allegiances are blurred as techniques are perfected, and Lei Kung becomes less certain who's friend and who's foe in each chapter. Fists fly, limbs are lost, and blood vessels burst in this tale of furious rivals, supernatural masters, walking corpses, and, above all, raging kung fu!

Kagan McLeod is from Toronto, Canada, and has enjoyed illustrating for newspapers, magazines, and design firms since 1999. His work had received awards from such groups as the Society of Newspaper Design, the Society of Illustrators of Los Angeles, American Illustration, and the Society of Publication Designers. He recommends *The Master of the Flying Guillotine* and *Boxer's Omen* wholeheartedly. The graphic novel *INFINITE KUNG-FU* will be his Top Shelf debut.

BB WOLF & THE 3 LP'S
J.D. Arnold & Rich Koslowski

A 2009 Release
88-Page Graphic Novel
ISBN 978-1-60309-029-2
Mature (16+)

From the award-winning creator of *THREE FINGERS* and *THE KING*, and the writing talents of J.D. Arnold, comes an all-new, pop culture thriller. Set in the Mississippi Delta of the 1920s, *B.B. WOLF & THE 3 LP'S* is a classic story of racial injustice, murder, revenge, and music — all told through the clever re-telling of a timeless fairy tale. … A farmer and family man by day, blues musician by night, and a drinker of fine spirits at any hour, B.B.'s life seemed simple. But this fragile peace comes crashing down when the LPs decide to take his land by any means possible. When all is lost, B.B. lashes out, setting into motion acts of revenge that only a big bad wolf could unleash.

J.D. Arnold has been hopelessly addicted to comic books since he could crawl. The first of many lifelong dreams came true in 2007 when he became part owner in his local comic book shop. The second comes true next year with the publication of his first comic related work, *B.B. WOLF & THE 3 LP'S*. He lives in Santa Cruz, California with his lovely wife Katie and his three fat and lazy cats.

Rich Koslowski has worked in the animation and comic book field for almost two decades. Not only is he an inker for Archie Comics and the self-publisher of the multiple Eisner-nominated comic book series, *The 3 Geeks* (a.k.a. Geeksville), he's also found the time to produce two graphic novels for Top Shelf: the Ignatz Award-winning *THREE FINGERS* , and *THE KING*. Rich lives in Wisconsin with his wife Sandy and their lovely little girl, Stella. His most recent work is the illustrated novella *The List*.

Money, Mississippi.
-1920-

"THEY SAY YOU GOTS TO SUFFER TO SING THE BLUES."

"WELL BROTHER, I HAVE SUFFERED. I HAVE SUFFERED LIKE NOBODY'S BUISNESS."

"GOT NOTHIN, GOT NOTHIN TO LOSE. RIGHT?"

"HUH. I HAD NOTHING AND I LOST IT ALL."

"AND I'D GIVE ANYTHING I COULD GET MY HANDS ON TO GET IT BACK AGAIN."

"BUT ALL I CAN GET MY HANDS ON IS THIS HERE GUITAR."

"SO I'LL SING THE BLUES..."

"ONE MORE TIME."

"IT ALL BEGAN, INNOCENTLY ENOUGH, ON A SUNDAY MORNING. THE NIGHT BEFORE HAD BEEN THE USUAL SCENE..."

"YOU SEE I MADE MY LIVING, MEAGER AS IT WAS, AS A FARMER. THAT'S HOW I FED MYSELF, THE MISSUS, AND TH' LITTLE 'UNS. HUH."

"RABID LITTLE PUPS RAN ME RAGGED AND COULD DRIVE ANY WOLF TO DRINK. EVEN IF HE DIDN'T HAVE PENCHANT FOR IT ALREADY... WHICH I DID."

BAM BAM BAM BAM

"BUT I LIVED BY THE BLUES. WELL, THAT AND DRINKING. AND THAT'S WHAT I MEANT BY THE USUAL SCENE."

BAM
BAM
BAM

"ANOTHER LATE NIGHT OF BOOZIN' AND BLUESIN', AND NOW I HAD TO WAKE UP TO THIS!?!"

KNOCK KNOCK KNOCK

WHAT IN BLAZES IS GOIN' ON HEAH!?
YA GUNNA STOP RIGHT THERE, MISTA.
YOU AIN'T GONNA TELL ME WHAT TA DO ON MY OWN FARM! NOW'S WHO'S GUNNA TELL ME WHAT IN THE NAME OF CREATION IS GOIN' ON HEAH!?

HEY, MISTER: COME HELL OR HIGHWATER PANTS

Pete Sickman-Garner

A 2009 Release

96-Page Graphic Novel

ISBN 978-1-60309-030-4

Mature (16+)

"We can't tell you how excited we are to have HEY, MISTER *back in action.* THE AFTER SCHOOL SPECIAL *was the very first graphic novel we published together, and we've been super-fans of the series since the early mini-comics. Get ready to have fun with this one."*

—Chris and Brett

Mister, Aunt Mary and Young Tim are back in a hellarious new adventure when they take in their old pal Satan as their new roomie. Tired of Hell's bleak landscape, Satan decides that maybe it's time he leave the underworld behind and join the upright citizens brigade — but before he can make a break for it, he's taken captive by a hostile coup of demons. Only Mister and the crew can save him, if they can find a way into Hell. With the help of a mysterious stranger (hint: It's Jesus!) they make it to the ninth circle and find Satan. But will they ever make it out? (Hint: Yes, except possibly for Tim).

Pete Sickman-Garner was born into a closed religious community in Michigan's Upper Peninsula. He and his older sister were raised by missionary parents dedicated to bringing word of the one true G*D to the darkest corners of the globe. A brief affair with his animist nanny forced a family rift (they were later reconciled in a ceremony televised nationally on the *700 Club*) and he spent his teenage years in Lusaka, Zambia waiting tables by day and soaking up the rich, cultural heritage in the bars and cafes at night. He made his way to Kuwait in 1991 and, hopping a ride with the 82nd Airborne, he returned to the States to begin a life of cartooning and scrimshaw just as the first Gulf War was coming to an end. While scrimshaw pays the bills, drawing comics will always be his first love.

Pete Sickman-Garner | 189

PERENNIALS

Here's a sampling of Top Shelf
creators and titles that should
already be on your (top) shelf.
Grab 'em up before they go
out of print, yet again!

Rare bookplate art. From Hell. Eddie Campbell

Featuring the ALL-AGES work of:

Andy Runton (OWLY)
Christian Slade (KORGI)
James Kochalka (PINKY & STINKY, MONKEY VS. ROBOT)
Aaron Renier (SPIRAL-BOUND)
Jef Czekaj (GRAMPA & JULIE)

... and the MATURE work of:

Alan Moore (LOST GIRLS, FROM HELL)
Craig Thompson (BLANKETS, CARNET DE VOYAGE)
Jeffrey Brown (CLUMSY, INCREDIBLE CHANGE-BOTS)
Alex Robinson (BOX OFFICE POISON, TRICKED)
James Kochalka (AMERICAN ELF, SUPERF*CKERS)
Robert Venditti & Brett Weldele (THE SURROGATES)
Jeff Lemire (TALES FROM THE FARM, GHOST STORIES)
Matt Kindt (SUPER SPY, 2 SISTERS)
Renée French (THE TICKING, MICROGRAPHICA)
Rich Koslowski (THE KING, THREE FINGERS)
Liz Prince (WILL YOU STILL LOVE ME IF I WET THE BED?)
Lilli Carré (TALES OF WOODSMAN PETE)
Jeremy Tinder (CRY YOURSELF TO SLEEP, BLACK GHOST APPLE FACTORY)
... plus many more!

ANDY RUNTON

OWLY

Winner of the Eisner Award for Best Publication for a Younger Audience, the Harvey Award for Best New Talent, the Ignatz Award for both Outstanding Series and Promising New Talent, and the Howard Eugene Day Memorial Prize — with over 100,000 graphic novels and 100,000 comics in circulation to date.

"Charming ... Expressive ... Appeals to all ages."

—People Magazine

"An incredibly sweet book ... perfect for give-and-take between children and their parents. Even readers older than the target audience will appreciate the book's simple charm, wisdom, and warmth."

—*Tina Coleman*, Booklist

"These deceptively simple stories portray a profound truth about the meaning of true friendship, loyalty, and faith. Younger elementary students can just enjoy the story, whereas older students and adults will see beyond the pictures to the underlying philosophy. This treasure of a book celebrates innocence and friendship and makes the reader feel wonderful in the end."

—*Kat Can*, Voice of Youth Advocates

Owly is a kind, yet lonely, little owl who's always on the search for new friends and adventure. The first graphic novel contains two enchanting novellas, "The Way Home" & "The Bittersweet Summer," wherein Owly discovers the meaning of friendship, and that saying goodbye doesn't always mean forever.

The second graphic novel follows Owly as he learns that sometimes you have to make sacrifices for things that are important, especially friendship.

The third graphic novel tells a charming story of understanding and acceptance, where Owly learns that everyone is special and it's okay to be different. And the fourth graphic novel tells the story of a new visitor to the forest — he may be misunderstood because of how he looks, but things aren't always what they seem, and everyone soon finds out that the power of friendship can fix just about anything.

Relying on a mixture of symbols, icons, and expressions to tell his silent stories, Runton's clean, animated, and heartwarming style makes it a perfect read for anyone who's a fan of Jeff Smith's *Bone* or Dav Pilkey's *Captain Underpants*. Don't miss the latest big thing in graphic novels!

OWLY (VOL 1): THE WAY HOME & THE BITTERSWEET SUMMER
160-Page Graphic Novel
ISBN 978-1-891830-62-4
Diamond Order Code: JUL043246

OWLY (VOL 2): JUST A LITTLE BLUE
128-Page Graphic Novel
ISBN 978-1-891830-64-8
Diamond Order Code: DEC042913

OWLY (VOL 3): FLYING LESSONS
144-Page Graphic Novel
ISBN 978-1-891830-76-1
Diamond Order Code: JUL053175

OWLY (VOL 4): A TIME TO BE BRAVE
128-Page Graphic Novel
ISBN 978-1-891830-89-1
Diamond Order Code: FEB073809

OWLY PLUSH TOY
Plush Toy
Diamond Order Code: AUG063613
$19.95 (US)
Ages 3 and up

CHRISTIAN SLADE

"In many ways, KORGI is a prime example of how to handle an all-ages book. With just the right level of surprise and adventure, it's determined to hook older readers just as quickly as children."
—Greg McElhatton, Read About Comics

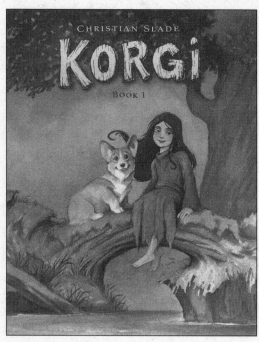

Christian Slade, a former Disney animator and currently full-time freelance illustrator, has brought to Top Shelf a gorgeously illustrated woodland fantasy about a young girl Ivy, her dog Sprout, and their amazing adventures in Korgi Hollow. In this first volume in the series, Ivy and Sprout discover some interesting things about themselves as they stray from their village and face danger for the first time. Perfect for fans of J.R.R. Tolkien's *The Hobbit*, Jeff Smith's *Bone*, or Andy Runton's *Owly*, *Korgi* is a charming all-ages epic that is sure to capture your heart.

KORGI (BOOK 1): SPROUTING WINGS!

88-Page Graphic Novel
ISBN 978-1-891830-90-7
Diamond Order Code: FEB073807
$10.00 (US)
Dimensions: 6 1/2" x 8 1/2"
All Ages

JAMES KOCHALKA

PINKY & STINKY

208-Page Graphic Novel
ISBN 978-1-891830-29-7
Diamond Order Code: STAR16037
$17.95 (US)
Dimensions: 8 1/2" x 8 1/2"
All Ages

"Oh, lord, did PINKY & STINKY *make me six years old again."*
—*Peter Aaron Rose,* Artbomb

Pinky and Stinky are fat little piglets, but just because they're cuties that doesn't mean they're not brave astronauts! Determinedly, they embark on a daring mission to be the first pigs on Pluto, but things go horribly wrong as soon as the journey begins and they crash land on the moon. Soon they find themselves playing a pivotal role in the Moon Men's battle to free themselves from the oppression of the American space program! This is an unabashedly fun book, like *Star Wars* mixed with *Pokemon*, if you can believe that!

MONKEY VS. ROBOT (VOL 1)

160-Page Graphic Novel
ISBN 978-1-891830-15-0
Diamond Order Code: MAR053223
$10.00 (US)
Dimensions: 6" x 6"
All Ages (10+)

MONKEY VS. ROBOT (VOL 2): THE CRYSTAL OF POWER

176-Page Graphic Novel
ISBN 978-1-891830-36-5
Diamond Order Code: STAR18507
$14.95 (US)
Dimensions: 8" x 8"
All Ages (10+)

"The MONKEY VS ROBOT books are like the best of children's literature, in that they appeal to the joyfulness of literature and art that appeals so much to children, while adults can enjoy the structure and techniques."

—Ninth Art

VOL 1: A factory of self-replicating robots is stripping the jungle of its natural resources, threatening the territory of a colony of nearby monkeys. A series of encounters between the two groups quickly escalates into all-out war. Beneath a charming and entertaining veneer runs a stirring examination of the dual nature of existence, the dichotomy within the human mind, and our profound effect on the ecological environment. A modern day fable exploring the age-old struggle between nature and technology.

VOL 2: Deep in the forest, robots are gathering plant and animal samples, and bringing them back to Mother Computer's Knowledge Extractor for analysis. When one spunky monkey breaks free of the device, a short circuit burns out the power Crystal in one of Mother's Cognitive Reactors. Now, the robots must find a replacement Crystal... but the one they dig up is a sacred relic from a monkey burial ground. Will the monkey's stand for that?

AARON RENIER

Winner of the Eisner Award for Talent Deserving Wider Recognition

SPIRAL-BOUND

184-Page Graphic Novel
ISBN 978-1-891830-50-1
Diamond Order Code: JUN053272
$14.95 (US)
Dimensions: 7 1/2" x 9 3/4"
All Ages (10+)

"Brilliant! Aaron Renier has created a playfully mysterious universe, complete with its own dreamlike logic. It's a delightfully inventive treasure."
—Dav Pilkey, author of Captain Underpants

"Aaron Renier's SPIRAL-BOUND is exactly the sort of novel I have been looking for."
—Lemony Snicket

"Top Shelf has a real winner with Aaron Renier's delightful, action-packed graphic novel for all ages."
—*Jeannine Wiese*, Ingram Library Services

With an ensemble cast straight from a box of Animal Crackers, this delightful tale of ambition, morality, and self-discovery is the first major work by extraordinary newcomer Aaron Renier. Drawn in a decidedly beautiful fashion reminiscent of Richard Scarry and Lewis Trondheim, Renier has given us a fully realized and compellingly adventurous narrative, at once both achingly naive and profoundly worldly. This tightly crafted graphic novel is the real deal, and will charm your socks off. A remarkable debut.

JEF CZEKAJ

GRAMPA & JULIE: SHARK HUNTERS
128-Page Full-Color Graphic Novel
ISBN 978-1-891830-52-5
Diamond Order Code: JUN042868
$14.95 (US)
Dimensions: 10" x 7 1/2" (landscape)
All Ages (6+)

"[Grampa and Julie's] escapades will delight kids who like the Sunday comics. Czekaj demonstrates a wonderful sense of the absurd ... and the results are hilarious. Parents reading this aloud will have as much fun as their children."

—Tina Coleman, Booklist

"This charming children's comic overflows with humor, adventure and whimsy. ... While youngsters will enjoy the breakneck pace and underwear gags, there's some level of satire for every age."

—Publishers Weekly

Equal parts *Tin Tin* and *The Simpsons*, this full-color graphic novel—suitable for children and adults of all ages—collects Jef Czekaj's endearing and delightful tale from the pages of *Nickelodeon Magazine* (which reaches over one million kids and parents each month). Join Julie and her world-famous Grampa in endless zany adventures as they search the high seas for Stephen, the largest shark in the world. Along the way they meet rapping squirrels, nerdy pirates, and entrepreneurial penguins as they travel from the bottom of the ocean to the furthest reaches of outer space. Will they find Stephen? Will pirates make them walk the plank? And will Julie ever get her Grampa to stop goofing around? Dive in and find out. Published in association with Nickelodeon, and funded in part by a grant from the Xeric Foundation.

ALAN MOORE

"You wouldn't necessarily think that an anarchist Gnostic who worships the Roman snake-god Glycon would be at the top of his field, but Alan Moore is universally acknowledged as the most important mainstream comics writerof the last three decades."
—*Douglas Wolk,* Slate

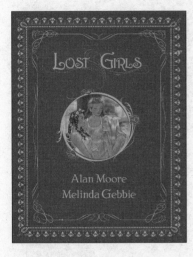

LOST GIRLS
by Alan Moore & Melinda Gebbie
Three, 112-Page, Super-Deluxe,
Ovesized Hardcover Volumes, Sealed In A
Slipcase
ISBN 978-1-891830-74-7
Diamond Order Code: JUN063440
$75.00 (US)
Dimensions: 9" x 12" x 2 1/2"
ADULTS ONLY

For more than a century, Alice, Wendy and Dorothy have been our guides through the Wonderland, Neverland and Land of Oz of our childhoods. Now like us, these three lost girls have grown up and are ready to guide us again, this time through the realms of our sexual awakening and fulfillment. Through their familiar fairytales they share with us their most intimate revelations of desire in its many forms, revelations that shine out radiantly through the dark clouds of war gathering around a luxury Austrian hotel. Drawing on the rich heritage of erotica, *LOST GIRLS* is the rediscovery of the power of ecstatic writing and art in a sublime union that only the medium of comics can achieve. Exquisite, thoughtful, and human, *LOST GIRLS* is a work of breathtaking scope that challenges the very notion of art fettered by convention. This is erotic fiction at its finest.

LOST GIRLS is packaged as three, 112-page, super-deluxe, ovesized hardcover volumes, all sealed in a gorgeous slipcase. Truly an edition for the ages.

LOST GIRLS

NAMED ONE OF "THE TOP 25 BEST BOOKS OF THE YEAR" BY THE VILLAGE VOICE:

"A beautiful dirty book ... LOST GIRLS is to erotic literature what Moore's now classic 1987 Watchmen *(with Dave Gibbons) was to the superhero scene. Each busts the frames of its respective genre with formal precision; each reflects upon its own ways and means through books within the book; and, most importantly, each kicks great writing into hyperdrive with dense and resonant imagery."*

—Richard Gehr

NAMED ONE OF "THE BEST GRAPHIC NOVELS OF THE YEAR" BY THE PUBLISHERS WEEKLY COMICS CRITICS POLL:

"What's more surprising? That Moore and Gebbie decided to explore the decidedly 'adult' exploits of some of literature's favorite young ladies, or that the result is as elegant and thought provoking as it is titillating?"

"As an exercise in the formal bounds of pure comics, LOST GIRLS is remarkable, as good as anything Moore has done in his career. ... Whatever you call it, there has never been anything quite like this in the world before, and I find myself extraordinarily pleased that someone of Moore's ability actually has written that sort of comics for adults."

—Neil Gaiman

"Moore's writing is clever, insightful, and layered with winning characterizations of aristocratic Alice, hoyden Dorothy, and repressed bourgeois Wendy. And his prose is matched by Gebbie's sumptuous art, with Matisse-like color and design that simultaneously suggest childhood and the fantasy elements of adult sexuality. This lavish confection is intellectually, aesthetically, and erotically intriguing, with no holds barred. For adult collections only."

—Martha Cornog, Library Journal

"The brilliance of the book is that it isn't harmless. Moore and Gebbie aren't just doing a giggly porno version of classic children's stories, they're retelling them with the fantasy removed, replaced by the coming-of-age experiences that were previously rendered as metaphor. ... LOST GIRLS' constant pull between arousal and disgust also makes for a reading experience that's as emotional as it is intellectual."

—Noel Murray, The Onion

Winner of the Eisner, Harvey, and Ignatz Awards for Best Graphic Novel

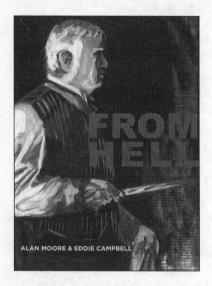

"My all-time favorite graphic novel ... an immense, majestic work about the Jack the Ripper murders, the dark Victorian world they happened in, and the birth of the 20th century."
—*Warren Ellis,*
Entertainment Weekly

FROM HELL

Alan Moore & Eddie Campbell
572-Page Graphic Novel
ISBN 978-0-9585783-4-9
Diamond Order Code: STAR16789
$35.00 (US)
Dimensions: 7 1/2" x 10" x 1 1/4"
Mature (18+)

FROM HELL is the story of Jack the Ripper, perhaps the most infamous man in the annals of murder. Detailing the events leading up to the Whitechapel killings and the cover-up that followed, *FROM HELL* is a meditation on the mind of a madman whose savagery and violence gave birth to the 20th century. The serialized story, presented in its entirety in this volume, has garnered widespread attention from critics and scholars, and has been adapted into a major motion picture from Twentieth Century Fox starring Johnny Depp and Heather Graham. Often regarded as one of the most significant graphic novels ever published, *FROM HELL* combines meticulous research with educated speculation, resulting in a masterpiece of historical fiction both compelling and terrifying. This new edition has been completely re-mastered, and is definitely the nicest edition of the book produced to date.

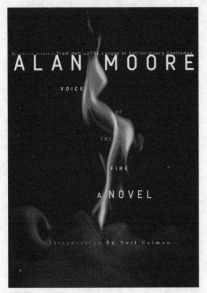

With an introduction by Neil Gaiman, thirteen color plates by José Villarrubia, and a dust jacket design by Chip Kidd

VOICE OF THE FIRE
ISBN 978-1-891830-44-0
Diamond Order Code: JUN032566
$26.95 (US)
Dimensions: 6 1/2" x 9 1/2"
Mature (16+)

"A burning bush of a novel full of earthy wonder and wisdom, VOICE OF THE FIRE *is a head-spinning trip down time's sacred whirlpool."*
—*Richard Gehr,* Village Voice

"Do not trust the tales, or the town, or even the man who tells the tales. Trust only the voice of the fire."
—*Neil Gaiman, from the Introduction*

In a story full of lust, madness and ecstasy, we meet twelve distinctive characters that lived in the same region of central England over the span of six thousand years. Their narratives are woven together in patterns of recurring events, strange traditions and uncanny visions. First, a cave-boy looses his mother, falls in love and learns a deadly lesson. He is followed by an extraordinary cast of characters: a murderess who impersonates her victim, a fisherman who believes he has become a different species, a Roman emissary who realizes the bitter truth about the Empire, a crippled nun who is healed miraculously by a disturbing apparition, an old crusader whose faith is destroyed by witnessing the ultimate relic, two witches — lovers — who burn at the stake. Each interconnected tale traces a path in a journey of discovery of the secrets of the land. ... In the tradition of Kipling's *Puck of Pook's Hill,* Schwob's *Imaginary Lives* and Borges' *A Universal History of Infamy,* Moore travels through history blending truth and conjecture in a novel that is dazzling, moving, sometimes tragic, but always mesmerizing.

"THE MIRROR OF LOVE *is a unique, beautiful and immensely powerful marriage of voice and vision, fact and feeling. Part testament, part history, part celebration, it belongs on everybody's bedside table, gay, straight or undecided. Wonderful."*
—*Clive Barker*

THE MIRROR OF LOVE
Alan Moore & José Villarrubia
136-Page Full-Color Hardcover
ISBN 978-1-891830-45-7
Diamond Order Code: OCT032748
$24.95 (US)
Dimensions: 8" x 8"
Mature (16+)

"The only way to go to war with hate is to love. THE MIRROR OF LOVE *is the great weapon in our arsenal. Not only does it elegantly and profoundly tell our history, it gives us a perfect reflection of our immense beauty. Moore and Villarrubia weave a remarkable tapestry, in words and images, that captures with precision the ecclesiastical and ecstatic capabilities of the human heart."*
—*Margaret Cho*

This masterpiece, an epic poem in prose, is a passionate love letter that beautifully recounts the history of same-sex love. Author Alan Moore takes us on a fascinating journey from prehistory to the present, revealing the hidden side of Western culture through the lives of its greatest creators. Sappho, Michelangelo, Shakespeare, Emily Dickinson, Oscar Wilde, and many others are woven into this rich, visceral piece described by *The Comics Journal* as a "vital, affecting piece of work ... exquisitely moving — not because it's a testament to same-sex love, but because it's a testament to love, period." This edition presents the poem fully illustrated by José Villarrubia, who has previously collaborated with Moore on his series Promethea and his novel *VOICE OF THE FIRE*. It also features a foreword by novelist Robert Rodi and an introduction by OBIE Award-winning playwright David Drake, as well as an index of historical characters, a selection of classic poems quoted in the text, and a bibliography. The result is a truly arresting volume that captures the spirit of Moore's poem while redefining the concept of a picture book for adults.

CRAIG THOMPSON

"BLANKETS *is a great American novel.*
—*Andrew D. Arnold,* TIME

"Thompson manages to explore adolescent social yearnings, the power of young love and the complexities of sexual attraction with a rare combination of sincerity, pictorial lyricism and taste."
—Publishers Weekly

Winner of the Eisner, Harvey, and Ignatz Awards for Best Graphic Novel and Best Cartoonist.

"Thought provoking and touching."
—Publishers Weekly

"This is a genuine graphic novel, with a universal appeal."
—*Gordon Flagg*, Booklist

"I thought it was moving, tender, beautifully drawn, painfully honest, and probably the most important graphic novel since Jimmy Corrigan."
—*Neil Gaiman*

BLANKETS
592-Page Graphic Novel
ISBN 978-1-891830-43-3
Diamond Order Code: STAR19060
$29.95 (US)
Dimensions: 6 1/2" x 9 5/8" x 1 1/2"
Mature (16+)

Wrapped in the landscape of a blustery Wisconsin winter, *BLANKETS* explores the sibling rivalry of two brothers growing up in the isolated country, and the budding romance of two coming-of-age lovers. A tale of security and discovery, of playfulness and tragedy, of a fall from grace and the origins of faith. A profound and utterly beautiful work.

CARNET DE VOYAGE
224-Page Graphic Novel
ISBN 978-1-891830-60-0
Diamond Order Code: NOV053229
$14.95 (US)
Dimensions: 5 1/2" x 7 1/2"
Mature (16+)

Craig Thompson spent three months traveling through Barcelona, the Alps, and France, as well as Morocco. Spontaneous sketches and a travelogue diary document his adventures and quiet moments, creating a raw and intimate portrait of countries, culture and the wandering artist.

JEFFERY BROWN

The Girlfriend Trilogy

"You can open to any page and find something unusually bare and honest about these stories. They're surprising, even though half the moments are ones you've probably experienced yourself. Hard trick to pull off."

—*Ira Glass*, This American Life

"Funny, sad, and a little embarrassing, Jeff Brown . . . delivers the look at real life that other forms of 'reality' entertainment falsely promise."

—*Andrew D. Arnold*, TIME

"A million little brilliant and honest moments..."

—*Wil Moss*, New City Chicago

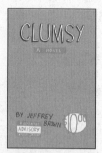

CLUMSY
232-Page Graphic Novel
ISBN 978-0971-3597-6-5
Diamond Order Code: STAR18186
$10.00 (US)
Dimensions: 4 1/2" x 7 1/4"
Mature (18+)

CLUMSY is the bittersweet story of a one-year, long-distance relationship, told through snippets of everyday life. Drawn in an elegantly awkward style that heightens the emotional impact and leaves you reminiscing about your own past love affairs, it also has a lot of sex.

UNLIKELY
256-Page Graphic Novel
ISBN 978-1-891830-41-9
Diamond Order Code: STAR19113
$14.95 (US)
Dimensions: 5" x 7 3/4"
Mature (18+)

A full-length graphic novel, *UNLIKELY* continues to explore the nature of relationships in excruciating detail and intimacy, in this story of how Jeffrey Brown lost his virginity.

AEIOU or ANY EASY INTIMACY
224-Page Graphic Novel
ISBN 978-1-891830-71-6
Diamond Order Code: APR053183
$12.00 (US)
Dimensions: 4" x 6"
Mature (18+)

AEIOU or *ANY EASY INTIMACY* continues to explore Jeffrey Brown's relationships themes, concentrating this time on the differences between knowing and loving someone, invoking the reader's relationship with the book as a parallel to being involved with someone.

"Brown is a consummate storyteller, with a mixture of believable dialogue that carries both wistful romance and casual cruelty... the longing gazes, the giddy feeling of being drunk, many different aspects of sex and a number of other subtle storytelling cues."
—Randy Lander, The Fourth Rail

"Mr. Brown seems to understand perfectly the day-to-day rhythms of the modern 'young adult' relationship. UNLIKELY, like his first book CLUMSY, is pretty much impossible to put down."
—Dan Clowes

EVERY GIRL IS THE END OF THE WORLD FOR ME
104-Page Graphic Novel
ISBN 978-1-891830-77-8
Diamond Order Code: FEB063347
$8.00 (US)
Dimensions: 5 1/4" x 5 1/4"
Mature (18+)

Autobiographical cartoonist Jeffrey Brown provides an epilogue to his Girlfriend "Trilogy," detailing the day-by-day events of a three-week run-in with five girls. Watch and be mesmerized by an ex coming back into the picture, a growing but poorly chosen crush, musings on the way friends come and go in life, and the realization that the end is never really the end.

INCREDIBLE CHANGE-BOTS
144-Page Full-Color Graphic Novel
ISBN 978-1-891830-91-4
Diamond Order Code: MAY073774
$15.00 (US)
Dimensions: 5" x 6 1/2"
Young Adult (13+)

Far away in space, there is a planet populated by machines able to change from robot form to vehicle form — the Incredible Change-Bots! Leaving their war torn planet, the Change-Bots arrive on Earth, where their battle continues — BUT AT WHAT COST?! Part parody, part nostalgic tribute, part moral fable, with *INCREDIBLE CHANGE-BOTS* Jeffrey Brown re-invents the shape changing robot genre into a heart stopping action comedy that's full of romance, half drama, and epic battles!

BIGHEAD
128-Page Graphic Novel
ISBN 978-1-891830-56-3
Diamond Order Code: AUG043100
$12.95 (US)
Dimensions: 6 1/2" x 9"
Mature (16+)

An irreverent and clever superhero parody, featuring the most amazing hero of all time: Bighead. Witness inept villains clash with an all-too-emotional hero, in the epic graphic novel that will leap all clichés in a single bound. *BIGHEAD* brings together moral fable, social commentary and classic comic book action, featuring a superhero who must save an unthankful world while facing the demons of his own failures.

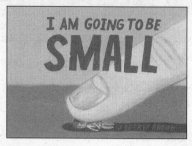

I AM GOING TO BE SMALL

384-Page Graphic Novel
ISBN 978-1-891830-86-0
Diamond Order Code: MAY063437
$14.00 (US)
Dimensions: 6 x 4 1/2"
Mature (18+)

Everyone needs something funny to stick in their pocket to read on the train, or on a lunch break, or in line at the DMV. This is that something. Jeffrey Brown sets aside the sappy sentimentality of his autobiographical comics to bring you this subtle and subversive, laugh-out-loud, giant-size, SMALL collection of gag cartoons.

MINISULK

96-Page Graphic Novel
ISBN 978-1-891830-66-2
Diamond Order Code:
JAN053031
$8.00 (US)
Dimensions: 4" x 6 1/4"
Mature (18+)

Jeffrey Brown takes a break from books about girls for this humorous short story collection featuring fiction, gags and autobiography. Included are such gems as "My Brother Knows Kung Fu" and "Action Television Show."

FEEBLE ATTEMPTS

48-Page Comic Book
Diamond Order Code: JAN073896
$5.00 (US)
Dimensions: 6 1/2" x 9"
Mature (16+)

Collecting some of Jeffrey Brown's favorite anthology and mini-comic stories, *FEEBLE ATTEMPTS* is at turns comedic and meaningful. It's densely packed with autobiographical musings, political jabs, Jesus, superheroes, funny job stories, childhood goofiness, and...okay, yes, even a little adolescent relationship drama. But only a little, we promise. Another essential addition to your comics library from one of today's funniest cartoonists.

BE A MAN

32-Page Comic Book
Diamond Order Code: DEC032717
$3.00 (US)
Dimensions: 4 5/8" x 7 1/4"
Mature (18+)

Jeffrey Brown's own self-parody of his "ultra-sensitive" graphic novel, *CLUMSY*. A heaping of in-your-face male chauvinism, over-the-top machismo, and self-involved gratification. For all those jerks who complained that Jeffrey Brown was a sissy, finally you can see him "Be a man!"

Also available: *CONVERSATIONS* #2, with James Kochalka (32-Page comic book.).

ALEX ROBINSON

**Winner of the Eisner Award for Talent
Deserving Wider Recognition, the International
Comics Festival Award for Best Debut Graphic
Novel (Angouleme, France), and voted by
Wizard Magazine as the Best Indy Graphic
Novel of All Time.**

BOX OFFICE POISON

608-Page Graphic Novel
ISBN 978-1-891830-19-8
Diamond Order Code: STAR13562
$29.95 (US)
Dimensions: 6 1/2" x 9 1/2"
Mature (18+)

*"Top Shelf Productions and Alex Robinson
have ruined me. Alex Robinson writes and
draws his own work. His original graphic
novels are long, slice of life stories, vital, fully
wrought and worth every moment spent
reading them. Top Shelf produces his work in
beautiful volumes. I fear opening the books,
because in addition to being beautiful, they
are intricate, true to life, and as it turns out,
full of impact. Now that I have read them,
there will be a new benchmark of success for
other books to reach."*
—Alex Ness, Pop Thought

*"A salute to comics, an exploration of the
human condition, and a solid, absorbing,
and riotously snide tale about at least half
of the things that make life important."*
—Tasha Robinson, The Onion

*"A convincing, absorbing and satisfying
fictional portrait of post-college life
in New York City."*
—Publishers Weekly

This epic story of Sherman, Dorothy, Ed, Stephen, Jane, and Mr. Flavor is a true
comics masterpiece. Alex Robinson's completely natural and inspiring knack for
dialogue makes this tale of dreary jobs, comic books, love, sex, messy apartments,
girlfriends (and the lack thereof), undisclosed pasts, and crusty old professionals one
of the most delightful and whimsical graphic novels to hit the stands in years.

Winner of the Harvey & Ignatz Awards for Best Graphic Novel

TRICKED

352-Page Graphic Novel
ISBN 978-1-891830-73-0
Diamond Order Code: JUN053269
$19.95 (US)
Dimensions: 6 1/2" x 9 1/2"
Mature (18+)

"Indy Book of the Year"

—Wizard Magazine

"Most indy film should be this good."

—Entertainment Weekly

"A drama and a thriller that plays to the real strength of the medium."

—Variety

"I've read a lot of excellent graphic novels this year, but I haven't read a better one than TRICKED. A wonderful piece of work about life and the mistakes we make and the demons that drive us."
—Heidi MacDonald,
Comic Buyers Guide

Four years in development and clocking in at 352-pages, Alex Robinson, "the master of true-to-life relationship drama" (*Library Journal*), has created another tour de force. *TRICKED* follows the lives of six people — a reclusive rock legend, a heartbroken waitress, a counterfeiter, an obsessive crank, a lost daughter, and a frustrated lover — whose lives are unconnected until an act of violence brings them spiraling in on each other. Combining intriguing characters with a story structure that is both complex and innovative, *TRICKED* is not to be missed.

BOP! [MORE BOX OFFICE POISON]

88-Page Graphic Novel
ISBN 978-1-891830-46-4
Diamond Order Code: STAR20107
$9.95 (US)
Dimensions: 6 1/2" x 9 1/2"
Mature (16+)

More *Box Office Poison* stories from Alex Robinson! What you might not know is that there were several short stories featuring Sherman, Ed, and friends, which were not included in the giant *BOX OFFICE POISON* collection. *BOP!* is an 88-page trade paperback reprinting all of those short stories including the *SPX Anthology* shorts, the *Box Office Poison Kolor Karnival* (seen here in glorious black and white), and some extra goodies.

"By basically transcribing a completely mental D&D session into comics — down to healing potions and backstabbing, which must be this week's theme — Alex Robinson's made the only Red Sonja comic I'd want to read."
—Kevin Church,
Beaucoupkevin.com

LOWER REGIONS
56-Page Graphic Novel
ISBN 978-1-60309-009-4
Diamond Order Code: SEP074014
$6.95 (US)
Dimensions: 4 1/2" x 6" (landscape)
Mature (16+)

The award-winning Alex Robinson follows up his acclaimed graphic novels with a bold new direction: a pretty barbarian lady with an axe chopping her way through a dungeon filled with monsters! And if that doesn't make you curious, how about this: this bloody, funny story contains only one word: THOOOOM! A unique blend of mayhem, cheesecake and humor, *ALEX ROBINSON'S LOWER REGIONS* will leave you breathless.

JAMES KOCHALKA

"Few people keep a diary as consistently and as entertainingly as James Kochalka. [His] tiny strips convey the personalities of him, his family and friends with astounding and impressive ease. Grade: A"
—Tom McLean, Variety

"Absolutely impossible to encapsulate into a single review, Kochalka's eminently likeable diary strips are a singular experience in the world of comics ... Comics' foremost optimist, Kochalka really distinguishes himself from his fellow cartoonists not only through deceptively simple and wonderful art, but also with a goofy, vulnerable cheerfulness. In a medium where many creators find life unbearably and predictably painful, he finds the extraordinary in the ordinary."
—4-Color Review

AMERICAN ELF (BOOK 1)
THE COLLECTED SKETCHBOOK DIARIES OF JAMES KOCHALKA
(October 26, 1998 to December 31, 2003)
520-Page Graphic Novel
ISBN 978-1-891830-49-5
Diamond Order Code: MAY042960
$29.95 (US)
Dimensions: 8 1/2" x 8 1/2"
Mature (16+)

Winner of the Ignatz Award for both Outstanding Comic & Outstanding Online Comic.

AMERICAN ELF (BOOK 2)
THE COLLECTED SKETCHBOOK DIARIES OF JAMES KOCHALKA (Jan. 1, 2004 to Dec. 31, 2005)
192-Page Full-Color Graphic Novel
ISBN 978-1-891830-85-3
Diamond Order Code DEC063936
$19.95 (US)
Dimensions: 8 1/2" x 8 1/2"
Mature (16+)

Kochalka's diaries have utterly redefined the daily comic strip. His attempt to document the minutia of his life results in work that explores the full spectrum of human emotions. Drawn with verve and confidence by a cartoonist at the height of his powers, it is ambitious, hilarious, moving, and quite addictive! These astounding books follow the ups and downs of Kochalka's life through seven full years of the strip. Quite simply, this is Kochalka's masterpiece. And be sure to visit americanelf.com to see the latest daily strips.

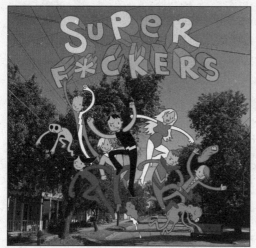

"SUPERF*CKERS is non-stop hijinx and fun; filthy, vulgar, explicit fun, and it cracks me up. I love ridiculousness, mockery and political un-correctness, and that's what this book seems to be all about."
—Justin Ponsor,
Comic Book Resources

"Kochalka expertly suggests what unchecked supernatural power would be like in the hands of the instant gratification generation. And it's funny, because anyone who remembers being a teen realizes what he or she would have been like with unchecked power."
—Leroy Douresseaux,
Comic Book Bin

No, it's not a sex book! The SUPERF*CKERS are the baddest teenage superhero team around, and everybody wants to join. They live in a big clubhouse, play video games on their state-of-the-art supercomputer, smoke their teammate Grotus' slime drippings, and fight amongst themselves like cats and dogs. Would-be heroes are lining up outside the door for a chance to try-out for a spot on the elite team. But why must they incessantly keep ringing the doorbell? The try-outs aren't until tomorrow. Somebody's got to stop them. This book is outrageously funny, vibrantly colored, and out of control. Just like America.

SUPERF*UCKERS

SUPERF*CKERS #1: 32 Pages, Diamond Order Code: MAR053221, $7.00 (US)
SUPERF*CKERS #2: 24 Pages, Diamond Order Code: AUG053230, $5.00 (US)
SUPERF*CKERS #3: 24 Pages, Diamond Order Code: APR063412, $5.00 (US)
SUPERF*CKERS #4: 24 Pages, Diamond Order Code: MAR073739, $5.00 (US)
All SUPERF*CKERS comics are 8" x 8" and rated Mature (18+)

Also available, featuring work by James Kochalka:
CONVERSATION #1 with Craig Thompson, comic book, $4.95
CONVERSATION #2 with Jeffrey Brown, comic book, $4.95
MAGIC BOY & ROBOT, graphic novel, $9.95
THE PERFECT PLANET, graphic novel, $14.95

ROBERT VENDITTI & BRETT WELDELE

"The Best Indy Book of the year. Sci-fi tales are making a comeback and THE SURROGATES *is quietly leading the charge."*
—*IGN*

"Robert Venditti delivers an impressive comics debut."
—*SFX*

THE SURROGATES 1.0
208-Page Full-Color Graphic Novel
ISBN 978-1-891830-87-7
Diamond Order Code: MAY063435
$19.95 (US)
Dimensions: 6 5/8" x 10 1/8"
Young Adult (13+)

SOON TO BE A MAJOR MOTION PICTURE!

The year is 2054, and life has been reduced to a data feed. The fusing of virtual reality and cybernetics has ushered in the era of the personal surrogate, android substitutes that let users interact with the world without ever leaving their homes. It's a perfect world, and it's up to Detectives Harvey Greer and Pete Ford of the Metro Police Department to keep it that way. But to do so they'll need to stop a techno-terrorist bent on returning society to a time when people lived their lives instead of merely experiencing them. In the tradition of William Gibson and Philip K. Dick, *THE SURROGATES* is more than just an action story with sci-fi trappings. Applying familiar tropes in unfamiliar ways, The Surrogates is about progress and whether there exists a tipping point at which technological advancement will stop enhancing and start hindering our lives. It is also a commentary on identity, the Western obsession with physical appearance, and the growing trend to use science as a means of providing consumers with beauty on demand. This volume collects all five issues of the critically-acclaimed comic book miniseries. Packed with bonus content, inside you will find never-before-seen sketches and artwork, as well as commentary from the creative team that brought this breakout story to the page.

JEFF LEMIRE

The Essex County Trilogy

WINNER OF THE AMERICAN LIBRARY ASSOCIATION/YALSA ALEX AWARD

ESSEX COUNTY (VOL 1): TALES FROM THE FARM
112-Page Graphic Novel
ISBN 978-1-891830-88-4
Diamond Order Code JAN073894
$9.95 (US)
Dimensions: 6 1/2" x 9"
Young Adult (13+)

ESSEX COUNTY (VOL 2): GHOST STORIES
224-Page Graphic Novel
ISBN 978-1-891830-94-5
Diamond Order Code JUL073879
$14.95 (US)
Dimensions: 6 1/2" x 9"
Young Adult (13+)

ESSEX COUNTY (VOL 3): THE COUNTRY NURSE
Shipping Fall 2008!
96-Page Graphic Novel
ISBN 978-1-891830-95-2
$9.95 (US)
Dimensions: 6 1/2" x 9"
Young Adult (13+)

"Books like this are the reason alternative comics publishers such as Top Shelf exist. Lemire uses an utterly personal, idiosyncratic drawing style, rough but completely clear, that even just-off-mainstream publishers would insist on gussying up for publication. And the simple story's slice-of-life lyricism, sparked by magic realism, is way too arthouse-movie-ish for the mainstream. But lordy, does it work!"
—*Ray Olson*, Booklist

"Jeff Lemire's TALES FROM THE FARM *is one of the best books I read last year, and I'm glad to see that it's finally coming out through a publisher that consistently brings interesting new talent to the fore. Lemire's going to go places, and I'm glad to get to watch him rise."*
—*Kevin Beaucoup*, Beacoupkevin.com

Essex County is the critically acclaimed (and absolutely amazing) trilogy of graphic novels from Xeric Award-winning cartoonist Jeff Lemire (Lost Dogs), set in a fictionalized version of his hometown of Essex County, Ontario.

Vol 1, *TALES FROM THE FARM* follows a recently orphaned 10-year-old who goes to live on his Uncle's farm. Their relationship grows increasingly strained, and Lester befriends the town's hulking gas station owner, Jimmy Lebeuf. The two escape into a private fantasy world of superheroes, alien invaders and good old-fashioned pond hockey.

Vol 2, *GHOST STORIES*, follows brothers Lou and Vince Lebeuf over the course of nearly seven decades. In it, eldest brother Lou, now a deaf and lonely man, lives out his final days on his farm full of guilt and regret for the decisions he made that tore his family apart. From their childhood on the farm to Toronto in the 1950s (where they both played professional hockey), Lou revisits his life, a silent observer haunted by his own memories.

Vol 3, *THE COUNTRY NURSE* follows a day in the life of Anne Morgan, the peculiar farming community's traveling nurse. As Anne checks in on her favorite patients, the story delves deeper into Essex County's mythology and past, and finally reveals how all three volumes stitch together to quilt a portrait of how loss and regret push and pull at the fabric of family in small town life.

MATT KINDT

SUPER SPY

336-Page Full-Color Graphic Novel
ISBN 978-1-891830-96-9
Diamond Order Code: JUN073913
$19.95 (US)
Dimensions: 5 3/4" x 8 1/4"
Young Adult (13+)

"This is a rip-roarin' yarn set in Europe during WWII about spies and assassins crossing paths — sometimes with lethal consequences. Fifty-odd short tales are all connected, telling a bigger story about love, betrayal, sudden death, loneliness and the stress of pretending to be someone you really aren't. Kindt's simple-but-stark art style suits a dark story taking place mostly in shadows. [...] Final word: A killer spy thriller."
—Dan Lennard, People Magazine (Australia)

"Matt Kindt's work on SUPER SPY blows my mind. The elegance of his art, juxtaposed with his rich character work, and complex narrative — is nothing short of genius. The Spy genre is so well-traveled, that sometimes it feels like everything's done before. But Matt Kindt's SUPER SPY proves that something new is always possible; if you unleash your passion, vision, and talent. Read SUPER SPY! Read 2 SISTERS! Read PISTOLWHIP! Buy Matt's art! I have. And my life is better for it!"
—Jesse Alexander,
Producer/Writer Heroes, Lost, and Alias

"Every now and then I get something really super-special from someone with so much talent....I can't describe accurately how handsome this book he's created is. You have to pick it up and hold it in your hands to see for yourself. So go get it and be amazed."
—Paul Malmont, author The Chinatown Deathcloud Peril

SUPER SPY is a super-deluxe, full-color collection of 52 interwoven spy thrillers about cyanide, pen-guns, heartbreak and betrayal. Spanning the countries of Spain, France, and Germany during World War II, each story follows the everyday life of a spy, exploring their small lies and deceptions, as well as the larger secrets they hide. A children's book is something more than it seems; a woman swims the English Channel to deliver a deadly secret; a German spy desperately seeks escape for herself and her daughter; and a spy continues to serve his country even beyond death. A gorgeous full-color graphic novel that not only reveals the nature of espionage, but how an individual can be lost in a world of lies and deception, and still manage to find redemption.

> *"There's enough swashbuckling, pen guns, cyanide teeth, buried treasure and nail-biting suspense to grip the interest of all readers."*
> —Wizard Magazine

2 SISTERS is a World War II spy thriller that spans both continents and centuries. From England to Spain, from ancient Rome through the era of pirates and buccaneers, this is the backdrop for the unique tale of two sisters, their relationship, and the secrets they share.

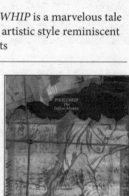

2 SISTERS
336-Page Graphic Novel
ISBN 978-1-891830-58-7
Diamond Order Code: APR042947
$19.95 (US)
Dimensions: 8 1/4" x 10 1/4" x 1"
Mature (16+)

ALSO AVAILABLE
by Matt Kindt & Jason Hall

A naïve bellhop's struggle towards a life's ambition; an expatriate musician on the run; a young woman's battle with her paranoia and her past; and the mysterious figure who wants to control their lives. Set in an exotic atmosphere of a bygone era, *PISTOLWHIP* is a marvelous tale crafted with a crime noir feel and an artistic style reminiscent of the best European graphic novelists

PISTOLWHIP
128-Page Graphic Novel
ISBN 978-1-891830-23-5
Diamond Order Code: STAR13698
$14.95 (US)
Dimensions: 8 1/2" x 10 1/2"
Young Adult (13+)

> *"PISTOLWHIP: THE YELLOW MENACE* is another genius entry in the *PISTOLWHIP* world created by writer Jason Hall and artist Matt Kindt. Blending the titular down-on-his-luck P.I., a beat cop, a radio show super-hero that may or may not be real, a crusader against comics, and a couple of dames, Hall and Kindt detonate their '50s influences in a terrific blast of mystery and meta-fiction."
> —*Troy Brownfield*,
> Shotgun Reviews

PISTOLWHIP:
THE YELLOW MENACE
144-Page Graphic Novel
ISBN 978-1-891830-35-8
Diamond Order Code: STAR17693
$14.95 (US)
Dimensions: 8 1/2" x 10 1/2"
Young Adult (13+)

MEPHISTO &
THE EMPTY BOX
24-Page Comic Book
Diamond Order Code: MAY012394
$3.95 (US)
Dimensions: 8 1/2" x 10 1/2"
Young Adult (13+)

On the night of their wedding, John and Carolyn Flynn attend the performance of a stage magician named Mephisto. But what dark and sinister secrets does Mephisto's devilish magic box hold for the newlyweds that will forever change their lives?

RENÉE FRENCH

"Nobody can touch Renée French for sweet fiendishness."
—Jim Woodring

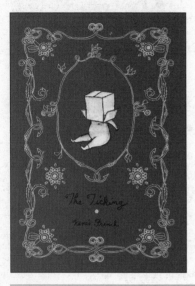

THE TICKING

216-Page Hardcover Graphic Novel
ISBN 978-1-891830-70-9
Diamond Order Code: FEB063346
$19.95 (US)
Dimensions: 5 1/2" x 8"
Mature (18+)

The story of Edison Steelhead, a boy who at birth takes his mother's life and his father's deformed face. Secreted away by his father to be raised in a remote island lighthouse, Edison relates to his surroundings in the only way he knows how — by capturing them in his sketchbook. Able to find beauty in even the most grotesque of things, Edison embraces his own unsettling appearance and sets out to confront the rest of the world. Waiting for him on its alien shores are the sights and experiences that will give shape to both his future and his past.

"A gem that means more with every reading."
—Booklist
"Renée French has long been one of my favorite artists and she doesn't disappoint in her latest work. Tiny creatures in tiny drawings with lots of crapballs makes this another freakish delight that also winds up being strangely touching."
—Jenna Fischer
(Pam, on NBC's The Office)

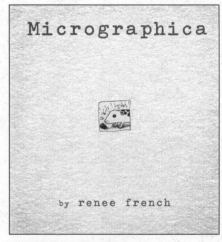

MICROGRAPHICA

208-Page Graphic Novel
ISBN 978-1-891830-93-8
Diamond Order Code: MAR073734
$10.00 (US)
Dimensions: 4 1/2" x 5"
Mature (16+)

A mob of tiny rodents live la vida loca, led by the bully Moe, and his trash-talking sidekick Preston. Add in Nubbins, the big guy; poor, sweet crapball-lovin' Aldo; and a rotting corpse turned playground, and you'll never find a more moving affirmation of traditional values. Inspired by a bald bird sighting while the author was wandering Hunter's Hill in Sydney, Australia, this book is pure weirdness — just what Renée French fans dream of. With guest drawings by Jim Woodring, Penn Jillette, Dean Cameron, Dylan Williams, James Gunn and more.

RICH KOSLOWSKI

"In the crowded and eclectic world of Elvis literature, once in a while, a breath of fresh air comes along to jolt our senses. Rich Koslowski's THE KING *is one of those rare entries which offers us something different, something which stimulates our senses both narratively and visually. ...* THE KING *well and truly takes care of business. Read, savour, and enjoy."*
— Nigel, Elvis Information Network

"Impressive ... a story about faith and the power of music and legend, as well as a lesson in how one man can become something larger than life."
—Randy Lander, The Fourth Rail

THE KING is an offbeat tale of one very enigmatic Elvis impersonator who's taking the Vegas strip, and the world, by storm. Shrouded in mystery with the shining gold helmet that covers his face, The King's performances are so mesmerizing that fans are starting to believe he really is Elvis Presley. Through investigative reporting and a series of thought-provoking interviews, a former tabloid journalist makes it his personal mission to find out The King's true identity. But in his race to debunk The King's latest comeback, he discovers much more than he bargained for.

THE KING
264-Page Two-Color Graphic Novel
ISBN 978-1-891830-65-5
Diamond Order Code: MAY053049
$19.95 (US)
Dimensions: 5 1/2" x 7 1/2"
Mature (16+)

Winner of the Ignatz Award for Best Graphic Novel

" . . . a single-minded obsession with animation history informs this work even as its creator twists and tears that history into a new, hideous, and hilarious form. There's a little bit of Roger Rabbit *and a whole lot of* Spinal Tap *at work here. Twisted and dark, funny and frightening, this is a deliciously evil toon history that demands attention."*
—Alan David Doanwe

Through a series of never-before-seen interviews and rare photos, documentary-maker Rich Koslowski reveals the horrifying true story behind the Cartoon industry and our most celebrated cartoon actors — the story that Hollywood doesn't want you to see. Told in the same style as a Ken Burns documentary, with interviews of 'toon stars today as well as historical "file footage" of the "early years," this work of fiction will forever change the way you think of those beloved characters in the white gloves.

THREE FINGERS
144-Page Two-Color Graphic Novel
ISBN 978-1-891830-31-0
Diamond Order Code: STAR16313
$14.95 (US)
Dimensions: 11" x 9" (landscape)
Mature (16+)

LIZ PRINCE

What started out as an exercise in keeping a personal comics journal quickly evolved into Liz Prince's first solo graphic novel. Described as a mix between Jeffrey

WILL YOU STILL LOVE ME IF I WET THE BED?

80-Page Graphic Novel
ISBN 978-1-891830-72-3
Diamond Order Code: JUL053179
$7.00 (US)
Dimensions: 4" x 6"
Mature (16+)

Brown and James Kochalka, Liz's comics are comprised of short vignettes that capture all the cute, gross, and endearing aspects of relationships. It's the perfect book for all those fans of autobiographical comics who want to see a happy ending.

"Beautifully simple and sweet, Liz prince portrays couples in a delightfully self-conscious way."
—*Farel Dalrymple*

"An adorable little collection of snippets and snapshots of moments from their relationship …
the silly, gross and snuggly moments that Liz and Kevin share.
A wondrous present to someone you hold dear."
—*Neil Figuracion,* Broken Frontier

LILLI CARRÉ

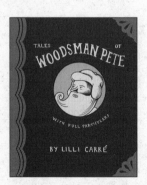

TALES OF WOODSMAN PETE

80-Page Graphic Novel
ISBN 978-1-891830-84-6
Diamond Order Code: APR063411
$7.00 (US)
Dimensions: 5 1/4" x 7 1/4"
Mature (16+)

"Lilli Carré's little book TALES OF WOODSMAN PETE *is really worth a look. It is, in its way, a heartbreaking little thing."*
—*Warren Ellis*

A collection of vignettes and stories about a solitary, albeit gregarious woodsman with a loose grasp on his own personal history and that of the outside world. He forms relationships with his inanimate surroundings and muses to a dead audience, specifically his bear rug, Philippe. His own tales eventually become entangled with that of the legendary Paul Bunyan, and the two become indirectly intertwined, illuminating the discrepancy between the character of the storyteller and the character within his stories. The lives of both Paul and Pete encounter such things as the questionable origin of an ocean, and the desire for preservation of everything from a fallen bird to an overused expression that has strayed a stone's throw from its original meaning.

JEREMY TINDER

"... adorable characters, a great sense of humor, and, at its core, very real emotions. Take a break from your Crisis on Infinite Civil Wars and discover a rabbit, a video store clerk and a robot worse off than you."
—Hilary Goldstein, IGN

"A tiny gem.
Tinder no doubt has a long career ahead of him."
—Troy Brownfield, Newsarama

CRY YOURSELF TO SLEEP
88-Page Graphic Novel
ISBN 978-1-891830-81-5
Diamond Order Code: MAR063449
$7.00 (US)
Dimensions: 4 1/2" x 6 1/2"
Young Adult (13+)

CRY YOURSELF TO SLEEP explores the disappointments of early adulthood by following the lives of three unique characters: Jim, a minimum wage rabbit struggling to pay his rent; Andy, an aspiring novelist dealing with rejection; and The Robot, a machine who just wants to be a better man. In this stellar debut graphic novel, Jeremy Tinder mixes sadness, sweetness and humor to tell a quirky little story of pride swallowing, fake moustaches, car crashes, and friendship.

BLACK GHOST APPLE FACTORY
48-Page Comic Book
Diamond Order Code: MAY073772
$5.00 (US)
Dimensions: 5" x 7 1/2"
Mature (16+)

BLACK GHOST APPLE FACTORY is a collection of mini-comics by Jeremy Tinder. Gathered from 2004-2006, these comics range from touching and somber to downright silly. In the title comic, a little black ghost has his head in the clouds at work, fixating on a hook-up from the previous evening. Another comic ends with the author, Tinder, having his face eaten by a grizzly bear. This volume is tiny, but tightly-packed with stories that will touch your heart and make you realize you're not the only one out there that has these thoughts running through your head. Also contains never-before-seen material.

NICOLAS MAHLER

LONE RACER

96-Page Two-Color Graphic Novel
ISBN 978-1-891830-69-3
Diamond Order Code: OCT063717
$12.95 (US)
Dimensions: 5 3/4" x 7 1/4"
Young Adult (13+)

"A sleeper of a book that deserves a wider audience ... a charming little gem."
—Chris Mautner, The Patriot-News

"LONE RACER is a refreshingly off-beat story, told in a unique graphic style. I love it!"
—Bill Plympton

LONE RACER is the story of a down-and-out racecar driver whose days of success are long gone. After a misguided attempt at a bank robbery — in which he is supposed to drive the getaway car — the Lone Racer decides that his days of going downhill are over. Will he get back on track?... A rare blend of whimsy and sadness, *LONE RACER* is a story of fast cars, faster women, and one man's ride from first to worst and back again.

"Mahler has succeeded in injecting human neuroses into the horror realm in a way that most other over-the-top comedians never broached. It resonates with the part of you that understands that even monsters need a dependable tavern in which to drown their sorrows, fears and foibles."
—Jarret Keene, Las Vegas Citylife

Austrian cartoonist Nicolas Mahler is famous for his silent and sophisticated comics. Perfect for fans of Edward Gorey, this volume includes humorous comics stories featuring the classic archetypes of the mummy, vampire, wolfman, Frankenstein, and, of course, Van Helsing. These short stories are intriguing, humorous, and incredibly illustrated in a whimsical, yet weighted, sketchy style.

VAN HELSING'S NIGHT OFF

112-Page Graphic Novel
ISBN 978-1-891830-38-9
Diamond Order Code: JAN042750
$12.95 (US)
Dimensions: 7 1/2" x 5 3/4" (landscape)
Mature (16+)

DAVID YURKOVICH

"I liked LESS THAN HEROES by David Yurkovich a lot, which means that I have now been tricked into liking a super-hero comic. F**k. … When done right, the super-hero genre can be an intelligent commentary on the way we both idealize and loathe ourselves, and Yurkovich manages to do this through a mixture of satire and random pop-culture references."
—Matt Speer, Too Much Coffee Man

In the city of Philadelphia there is a tall building at 18th and Market Street, atop of which live four individuals. As the official protectors of the city, their job is to be around when traditional law enforcement fails. But are they really heroes? Meet Philadelphia's contracted super-hero team, Threshold. A quartet more interested in milk and cookies than crime and punishment. A team more concerned with battling indigestion than their arch enemies. Sure, they have super-powers. They can leap tall buildings, fly, and do all the stuff other heroes do. More than human? Probably. Less than heroes? Without a doubt.

LESS THAN HEROES
152-Page Graphic Novel
ISBN 978-1-891830-51-8
Diamond Order Code: APR042942
$14.95 (US)
Dimensions: 6 1/2" x 10 1/2"
Mature (16+)

"If there have to be superhero comics, then I want them to be David Yurkovich's."
—Warren Ellis

Agent Swete — an unlikely hero comprised of organic chocolate and a member of the FBI's Food Crimes Division — and his sharp-tongued partner, Anderson,

investigate a series of bizarre, food-inspired crimes. Along the way they encounter a variety of characters including an extraterrestrial canine named Geoffrey, writer Ernest Hemingway, an organized crime lord intent upon finding the life-enabling 'eternity pasta,' and an eerie, all-devouring trio known as The Metabolators.

DEATH BY CHOCOLATE: REDUX
120-Page Graphic Novel
ISBN 978-1-891830-92-1
Diamond Order Code: APR074010
$14.95 (US)
Dimensions: 6 1/2" x 10 1/2"
Young Adult (13+)

PETE SICKMAN-GARNER

"America's funniest comic book."
—*Gavin Edwards,* Details

"Hey, Mister comics are laugh-out-loud, tears-rolling-down-your-face funny."
—*Karon Flage,* Sequential Tart

"Sickman-Garner's best work shows a complexity of vision and cartooning talent that make him eminently watchable; qualities which belie the seeming hopelessness of his work."
—The Comics Journal

The *AFTER SCHOOL SPEICAL* collects the original five, self-published *HEY, MISTER* mini-comics. With all the disturbing pathos and blow-milk-through-your-nose comedy we've come to expect, this cool compendium is guaranteed to give you the most for your hard-earned clamshells.

HEY, MISTER (VOL 1): AFTER SCHOOL SPECIAL
96-Page Graphic Novel
ISBN 978-1-891830-02-0
Diamond Order Code: STAR14243
$7.95 (US)
Dimensions: 5 3/8" x 8 1/4"
Mature (16+)

THE CELEBRITY ROAST collects the first four issues of Pete Sickman-Garner's regular series, *HEY, MISTER,* topped off with three new stories and a few anthology pieces. Follow the adventures of Pete's hilarious cast of misfits, Young Tim, Mister, Aunt Mary, and Hideous Mutants (don't ask!), as they continue their guerrilla war against everything sacred and beautiful — Best of all, there aren't any actual celebrities. Well, except for Sting, but he gets killed off rather quickly.

HEY, MISTER (VOL 2): THE CELEBRITY ROAST
144-Page Graphic Novel
ISBN 978-1-891830-06-8
Diamond Order Code: STAR14244
$9.95 (US)
Dimensions: 6" x 9"
Mature (16+)

THE FALL COLLECTION collects issues #5 thru #8 of the seven-time Eisner and Ignatz Award-nominated series. It includes *Behind The Green Door, The Trouble With Jesus, Eyes On The Prize,* and *Dial 'M' for Mister,* and as a bonus, also includes Sickman-Garner's cartoon account of who he is and why he does what he does.

HEY, MISTER (VOL 3): THE FALL COLLECTION
176-Page Graphic Novel
ISBN 978-1-891830-25-9
Diamond Order Code: STAR15108
$12.95 (US)
Dimensions: 6" x 9"
Mature (16+)

ANDY HARTZELL

"Andy Hartzell realizes a lot in his graphic novel, and anyone lucky enough to read FOX BUNNY FUNNY *will find a work of fiction that challenges the reader to think not only about himself, but also about his relationship to his own group and others. A gay/lesbian coming of age story, the Rwandan genocide, Sudan, American slavery, the Holocaust, the consumer economy, the food chain, gender transformation, identity politics —
the possibilities through which to view this story are endless."*
—*Leroy Douresseaux,* Comic Book Bin

FOX BUNNY FUNNY

104-Page Graphic Novel
ISBN 978-1-891830-97-6
Diamond Order Code: APR074013
$10.00 (US)
Dimensions: 6 1/2" x 9"
Mature (16+)

The rules are simple: you're either a fox or a bunny. Foxes oppress and devour, bunnies suffer and die. Everyone knows their place. Everyone's satisfied. So what happens when a secret desire puts you at odds with your society? Starting from a simple premise — and without using a single word — *FOX BUNNY FUNNY* leads the reader on a zigzag chase in and out of rabbit holes, and through increasingly strange landscapes where funny animals have serious identity problems. The tale swerves from slapstick to horror and back again before landing at the inevitable climax, in which all the old rules are shattered. When you emerge, you'll find yourself gazing at our own fragmenting society with new eyes.

SCOTT MORSE

"As a fan of Kurosawa and Morse and movies and comic books, this is about all I could ask for."
—*Scott Mosier, Producer of* Clerks

A BAREFOOT SERPENT

128-Page Graphic Novel (16 in full-color)
ISBN 978-1-891830-37-2
Diamond Order Code: STAR19511
$14.95 (US)
Dimensions: 6 3/4" x 8"
Mature (16+)

A heartwarming story of a young girl befriended by an extraordinary boy, as her family recovers from a tragedy while on vacation in Hawaii. Their lives are forever changed as they explore the island and themselves. Swimming in themes of loss and loneliness, as well as happiness and hope, this genuinely touching tale is book-ended by a full-color rumination on the life and work of legendary Japanese filmmaker, Akira Kurosawa. In this unique format, the central story's themes reflect those of the filmmaker — told through B&W half-toned, fully painted art — creating an absolutely beautiful and powerful masterpiece of contemporary biographical fiction.

CHRIS STAROS

YEARBOOK STORIES: 1976-1978
Chris Staros (with Bo Hampton and
Rich Tommaso)
32-Page Comic Book
Diamond Order Code: AUG074029
$4.00 (US)
Dimensions: 6 1/2" x 9"
Mature (16+)

"Great, truthful little moments and a genuinely
reflective conclusion leave the reader with real insight
into Staros' personality — hell, even into his
inclusive vision of comics."
—Alan David Doane, Comic Book Galaxy

"Chris Staros captures something here, and while other people might not see it, it is
really important. There is truth in what he writes, there is a sense of telling a reality
without being maudlin or hyperbolic, and you see inside his heart.
Of all the books I've read about school days, this one made me feel normal,
instead of estranged, it was pleasant even when uneasy,
and did not over-dwell in the crap of life. It just was."
—Alex Ness, Pop Thought

YEARBOOK STORIES: 1976-1978 features two autobiographical stories from
Chris Staros' formative High School years: "The Willful Death of a Stereotype,"
illustrated by Bo Hampton, and
"The Worst Gig I Ever Had,"
illustrated by Rich Tommaso.
Originally featured in the 2001
Small Press Expo Anthology
and nominated for the 2002 Eisner award for Best
Short Story of the Year, "The Willful Death of a
Stereotype" chronicles the events that led up to
a critical moment in Chris' high school life. And
originally featured in the 1999 Small Press Expo
Anthology, "The Worst Gig I Ever Had" deals with
one of the wildest rock'n'roll gigs ever — from
Chris' very first hard rock band.

COMIC BOOK ARTIST

Edited by Jon B. Cooke

WINNER OF THE EISNER AND HARVEY AWARDS FOR BEST COMICS-RELATED PERIODICAL.

Back issues of *COMIC BOOK ARTIST*, the multiple award-winning magazine devoted to the love of comics old and new, are still available. Supplies are short, so be sure to get caught up on all the issues as soon as you can.

COMIC BOOK ARTIST (VOL 2) #1 (featuring Neal Adams & Alex Ross):
128 Pages, Diamond Order Code: APR032554, $7.50 (US)

COMIC BOOK ARTIST (VOL 2) #2 (featuring Frank Cho):
112 Pages, Diamond Order Code: MAY032544, $7.50 (US)

COMIC BOOK ARTIST (VOL 2) #3 (featuring Darwyn Cooke):
112 Pages, Diamond Order Code: JAN042881, $7.50 (US)

COMIC BOOK ARTIST (VOL 2) #4 (featuring Alex Niño):
112 Pages, Diamond Order Code: MAR042971, $7.50 (US)

COMIC BOOK ARTIST (VOL 2) #5 (featuring Howard Chaykin):
112 Pages, Diamond Order Code: MAY043054, $7.50 (US)

COMIC BOOK ARTIST (VOL 2) #6 (featuring Will Eisner):
192 Pages, Diamond Order Code: APR053289, $14.50 (US)

APPENDIX I:

A BRIEF HISTORY OF TOP SHELF PRODUCTIONS

Brett Warnock began publishing graphic novels and comics in 1995 with the anthology *TOP SHELF*. Created in the spirit of promoting the careers of up-and-coming cartoonists, the anthology grew in scope and size, garnering critical accolades, as well as Best Anthology nominations from both the Harvey and Ignatz Awards. Publication of several other books followed, and Top Shelf began its reputation as a leader in discovering and showcasing the vanguard of the alternative comics scene. During this time, Chris Staros was gaining his own acclaim as the American agent for several international cartoonists (such as Eddie Campbell and Gary Spencer Millidge), as well as for being the author of *THE STAROS REPORT*, an annual hundred-page resource guide dedicated to discussing the most intelligent and innovative comics in the industry. *THE STAROS REPORT* also garnered a Best Comics-Related Periodical nomination from the Harvey Awards, as well two nominations from the prestigious Eisner Awards.

Brett and Chris first became friends, and then, at the Small Press Expo (SPX) in 1997, decided to become publishing partners in the newly formed Top Shelf Productions, Inc. Since that time, Top Shelf Productions has published over 175 graphic novels and comic books that have helped to revitalize interest in comics as a literary art form. Most notably, Alan Moore & Melinda Gebbie's *LOST GIRLS*, Alan Moore & Eddie Campbell's *FROM HELL*, Andy Runton's *OWLY*, Craig Thompson's *BLANKETS* and *CARNET DE VOYAGE*, and Jeffrey Brown's *CLUMSY* and *UNLIKELY*, which have garnered critical accolades from the likes of *TIME,*

Art by Max Estes

USA Today, *Entertainment Weekly*, *People Magazine*, *Publishers Weekly*, *The New Yorker*, and the *New York Times Book Review*. Perennial favorites also include: Alex Robinson's *BOX OFFICE POISON* and *TRICKED*; Renée French's *THE TICKING*; James Kochalka's *AMERICAN ELF* and *SUPERF*CKERS*; Jeff Lemire's Essex County Trilogy; Matt Kindt's *SUPER SPY*; Christian Slade's *KORGI*; and Robert Venditti & Brett Weldele's *THE SURROGATES*.

The future promises stellar new releases sure to appeal to both connoisseurs of superb narrative art and fans of engaging pop culture, as the Top Shelf line of books are ideally suited to attract new readers into the comicsphere. Keep an eye out for Alan Moore & Kevin O'Neill's *THE LEAGUE OF EXTRAORDINARY GENTLEMAN (VOL III): CENTURY*; Pat Mills & Kevin O'Neill's *MARSHAL LAW (OMNIBUS)*; Craig Thompson's *KISSYPOO GARDEN*; Eddie Campbell's *ALEC (LIFE-SIZE OMNIBUS)* and *BACCHUS (TWO-VOLUME OMNIBUS)*; Alex Robinson's *TOO COOL TO BE FORGOTTEN*; James Kochalka's *JOHNNY BOO*; Brian Ralph's CRUM BUMS; Nate Powell's *SWALLOW ME WHOLE*; Brian Wood and Nikki Cook's *DOGS DAY END*; Ray Fawkes & Vince Locke's *JUNCTION TRUE*; Kagan McLeod's *INFINITE KUNG-FU*; and our very first grimoire, *THE MOON & SERPENT BUMPER BOOK OF MAGIC* co-written by Alan Moore & Steve Moore.

We have many more books in print and available, so peruse our online catalog for an even larger glimpse of the incredible universe of comics available from Top Shelf, including work by Christian Slade, Aaron Renier, Jef Czekaj, Rich Koslowski, Liz Prince, Lilli Carré, Jeremy Tinder, Nicolas Mahler, David Yurkovich, Andy Hartzell, Scott Morse, Max Estes and many more. The bar is stocked, and the bartender is in.

APPENDIX II:
TOP SHELF PUBLISHING SCHEDULE

Here's a complete list of everything published and distributed by Top Shelf — including the proposed 2008 schedule!

2008 (PLANNED SO FAR — SUBJECT TO CHANGE)

Jan OWLY (VOL 4): A TIME TO BE BRAVE by Andy Runton
Jan OWLY (VOL 4): A TIME TO BE BRAVE (Hardcover) by Andy Runton
Jan 3rd Printing of OWLY (VOL 1): THE WAY HOME & THE BITTERSWEET SUMMER
Jan OWLY (VOL 1): THE WAY HOME & THE BITTERSWEET SUMMER (HC) by Runton
Jan The United Kingdon/European Union Release of LOST GIRLS

Feb DISCOVERED Edited by John Lowe (distributed)

Mar HIERONYMUS B. by Ulf K.

Apr THAT SALTY AIR by Tim Sievert
Apr TONOHARU: PART ONE by Lars Martinson (distributed)
+
Apr TOP SHELF SEASONAL SAMPLER — 2008 Edited by Chris Staros & Brett Warnock

May DELAYED REPLAYS by Liz Prince
May 24x2 by David Chelsea
May 2nd Printing of THE SURROGATES 1.0 by Robert Venditti & Brett Weldele
+
May OWLY & FRIENDS (FREE COMIC BOOK DAY) by Runton, Slade, Kochalka & Barba

Jun JOHNNY BOO (BOOK 1): THE BEST LITTLE GHOST IN THE WORLD by Kochalka
Jun 2nd Printing of ESSEX COUNTY (VOL 1): TALES FROM THE FARM by Jeff Lemire
Jun 2nd Printing of SUPER SPY by Matt Kindt
Jun 2nd Printing of WILL YOU STILL LOVE ME IF I WET THE BED? by Liz Prince

Jul TOO COOL TO BE FORGOTTEN by Alex Robinson
Jul YAM by Corey Barba
Jul 2nd Printing of PINKY & STINKY by James Kochalka

Aug KORGI (BOOK 2): THE COSMIC COLLECTOR by Christian Slade
Aug OWLY (VOL 5): TINY TALES by Andy Runton
Aug HOW TO LOVE by Actus Independent Comics

Sep SWALLOW ME WHOLE by Nate Powell
Sep VEEPS by Bill Kelter & Wayne Shellabarger
Sep SULK (VOL 1) by Jeffrey Brown

Oct ESSEX COUNTY (VOL 3): THE COUNTRY NURSE by Jeff Lemire
Oct CRUM BUMS by Brian Ralph
Oct COMIC BOOK ARTIST (VOL 2) #7: PETER BAGGE Edited by Jon Cooke

Nov LITTLE PAINTINGS by James Kochalka
Nov AMERICAN ELF (BOOK 3) by James Kochalka

Dec JOHNNY BOO (BOOK 2): TWINKLE POWER by James Kochalka
Dec COMIC BOOK ARTIST (VOL 2) #8: TONY HARRIS Edited by Jon Cooke
Dec SULK (VOL 2) by Jeffrey Brown

FUTURE RELEASES (FOR 2009 & 2010):

THE LEAGUE OF EXTRAORDINARY GENTLEMAN (VOL III): CENTURY
    by Alan Moore & Kevin O'Neill (A 3-Part Prestige-Format Series)
THE MOON & SERPENT BUMPER BOOK OF MAGIC
    by Alan Moore, Steve Moore, and various artists (A Super-Deluxe Grimoire — for Kids!)
MARSHAL LAW (OMNIBUS) by Pat Mills & Kevin O'Neill
KISSYPOO GARDEN by Craig Thompson
THE SURROGATES 2.0: FLESH & BONE by Venditti & Weldele
THE HOMELAND DIRECTIVE by Robert Venditti & Kristian Donaldson
ALEC (LIFE-SIZE OMNIBUS) by Eddie Campbell
BACCHUS (TWO-VOLUME OMNIBUS) by Eddie Campbell
THE MAN WHO LOVED BREASTS by Rob Goodin
DOGS DAY END by Brian Wood & Nikki Cook
JUNCTION TRUE by Ray Fawkes & Vince Locke
INFINITE KUNG-FU by Kagan McLeod
SECOND THOUGHTS by Niklas Asker
BB WOLF & THE 3 LP'S by J.D. Arnold & Rich Koslowski
HEY, MISTER: COME HELL OR HIGHWATER PANTS by Pete Sickman-Garner
VENUS: THE SECRET COMICS OF ARTHUR HOLLY by Dylan Horrocks
PINOKIO by Kurt Wolfgang
BRASS TACKS by Vincent Stall
LYRICAL WHALES by Scott Morse
The Next TOP SHELF SEASONAL SAMPLER Edited by Chris Staros & Brett Warnock
The Next OWLY by Andy Runton
The Next KORGI by Christian Slade
The Next JOHNNY BOO by James Kochalka
The Next YAM by Corey Barba
The Next AMERICAN ELF by James Kochalka
The Next SUPERF*CKERS by James Kochalka
The Next CONVERSATION by James Kochalka & Guest
The Next TONOHARU by Lars Martinson
The Next COMIC BOOK ARTIST Edited by Jon B. Cooke
… and several other projects still under wraps!

2007

Jan 3rd Printing of LOST GIRLS by Moore and Gebbie
Jan LONE RACER by Nicolas Mahler
Jan REGARDS FROM SERBIA by Aleksandar Zograf
Jan ARE WE FEELING SAFE AGAIN? (TH)INK by Keith Knight (distributed)
Feb AMERICAN ELF (BOOK 2) by James Kochalka
Feb OUR MOST BELOVED CD by James Kochalka Superstar (distributed)
Feb SPREAD YOUR EVIL WINGS AND FLY CD by James Kochalka Superstar (distributed)
Mar ESSEX COUNTY (VOL 1): TALES FROM THE FARM by Jeff Lemire
Mar FEEBLE ATTEMPTS by Jeffrey Brown
Mar PENCIL FIGHT #3 Edited by Bwana Spoons (distributed)
Apr KORGI (BOOK 1): SPROUTING WINGS! by Christian Slade
Apr KORGI (BOOK 1): SPROUTING WINGS! (Hardcover) by Slade
Apr 2nd Printing of OWLY (VOL 3): FLYING LESSONS by Andy Runton
May OWLY: HEPING HANDS (FREE COMIC BOOK DAY) by Andy Runton & Christian Slade
May TOP SHELF SEASONAL SAMPLER — 2007 Edited by Chris Staros & Brett Warnock
May TOP SHELF 10TH ANNIVERSARY POSTER by Ulana Zahajkewycz
May MICROGRAPHICA by Renée French
May SUPERF*CKERS #4 by James Kochalka
May 3rd Printing of UNLIKELY by Jeffrey Brown
May 8th Printing of BLANKETS by Craig Thompson
May 8th Printing of FROM HELL by Alan Moore & Eddie Campbell
Jun FOX BUNNY FUNNY by Andy Hartzell
Jun DEATH BY CHOCOLATE: REDUX by David Yurkovich
Jun DEE VEE 2007 Edited by Daren White
Jul INCREDIBLE CHANGE-BOTS by Jeffrey Brown
Jul INCREDIBLE CHANGE-BOTS (Hardcover) by Jeffrey Brown
Jul BLACK GHOST APPLE FACTORY by Jeremy Tinder
Aug SUPER SPY by Matt Kindt
Aug SUPER SPY (Hardcover) by Matt Kindt
Sep ESSEX COUNTY (VOL 2): GHOST STORIES by Jeff Lemire
Sep ELFWORLD (VOL 1) Edited by François Vigneault & Compiled by Brown (distributed)
Sep 2nd Printing of AEIOU by Jeffrey Brown
Oct YEARBOOK STORIES: 1976-1978 by Chris Staros (with Bo Hampton & Rich Tommaso)
Oct TROUBLETOWN TOLD YOU SO by Lloyd Dangle (distributed)
Nov LOWER REGIONS by Alex Robinson — 175th Publication!
Nov WORLD WAR 3 ILLUSTRATED #38: FACTS ON THE GROUND (distributed)

2006

Jan OWLY (VOL 3): FLYING LESSONS by Andy Runton
Jan THE SURROGATES #4 (of 5) by Robert Venditti & Brett Weldele
Jan 6th Printing of BLANKETS by Craig Thompson
Jan 2nd Printing of CARNET DE VOYAGE by Craig Thompson
Jan 2nd Printing of TRICKED by Alex Robinson
Feb COFFEE & DONUTS by Max Estes
Feb 2nd Printing of OWLY (VOL 1): THE WAY HOME & THE BITTERSWEET SUMMER
Feb 4th Printing of BOX OFFICE POISON by Alex Robinson
Mar THE SURROGATES #5 (of 5) by Robert Venditti & Brett Weldele
Mar OWLY T-SHIRTS by Andy Runton
Apr THE TICKING by Renée French
Apr EVERY GIRL IS THE END OF THE WORLD FOR ME by Jeffrey Brown

May OWLY: BREAKIN' THE ICE (FREE COMIC BOOK DAY) by Andy Runton
May 110 PER¢ by Tony Consiglio
May CRY YOURSELF TO SLEEP by Jeremy Tinder
Jun SUPERF*CKERS #3 by James Kochalka
Jun TALES OF WOODSMAN PETE by Lilli Carré
Jul I AM GOING TO BE SMALL by Jeffrey Brown
Jul I AM GOING TO BE SMALL (Hardcover) by Jeffrey Brown
Jul THE SURROGATES 1.0 by Robert Venditti & Brett Weldele
Aug LOST GIRLS by Alan Moore and Melinda Gebbie
Aug OWLY PLUSH TOY by Andy Runton (Top Shelf's First Toy!)
Sep 2nd Printing of OWLY (VOL 2): JUST A LITTLE BLUE by Andy Runton
Sep 5th Printing of CLUMSY by Jeffrey Brown
Sep 7th Printing of BLANKETS by Craig Thompson
Oct 2nd Printing of LOST GIRLS by Alan Moore and Melinda Gebbie
Oct 7th Printing of FROM HELL by Alan Moore & Eddie Campbell
Oct FROM HELL (Hardcover) by Alan Moore & Eddie Campbell
Oct HONEY TALKS by Stripburger (Boxed Set) (distributed)
Nov PLEASE RELEASE by Nate Powell
Nov WORLD WAR 3 ILLUSTRATED #37: UNNATURAL DISASTERS (distributed)

2005
Feb OWLY (VOL 2): JUST A LITTLE BLUE by Andy Runton
Feb MINIBURGER: DIRTY DOZEN by Stripburger (distributed)
Feb 3rd Printing of CREATURE TECH by Doug TenNapel
Feb 6th Printing of GOOD-BYE, CHUNKY RICE by Craig Thompson
Feb 5th Printing of BLANKETS by Craig Thompson
Mar MINISULK by Jeffrey Brown
Mar HELLO, AGAIN by Max Estes
Apr MOSQUITO by Dan James
Apr BUGHOUSE (VOL 3): SCALAWAG by Steve Lafler
May SUPERF*CKERS #1 by James Kochalka
May New Edition of MONKEY VS. ROBOT by James Kochalka
May OWLY: SPLASHIN' AROUND (FREE COMIC BOOK DAY) by Andy Runton
Jun AEIOU by Jeffrey Brown
Jun PENCIL FIGHT #2 Edited by Bwana Spoons
Jun 2nd Printing of SAME DIFFERENCE by Derek Kirk Kim
Jul THE SURROGATES #1 (of 5) by Robert Venditti & Brett Weldele
Jul THE KING by Rich Koslowski
Jul THE KING (Hardcover) by Rich Koslowski
Jul 4th Printing of CLUMSY by Jeffrey Brown
Jul 2nd Printing of UNLIKELY by Jeffrey Brown
Aug TRICKED by Alex Robinson
Aug TRICKED (Hardcover) by Alex Robinson
Aug New Edition of BOX OFFICE POISON by Alex Robinson
Aug New Edition of BOX OFFICE POISON (Hardcover) by Alex Robinson
Aug SPIRAL-BOUND by Aaron Renier
Sep THE SURROGATES #2 (of 5) by Robert Venditti & Brett Weldele
Sep WILL YOU STILL LOVE ME IF I WET THE BED? by Liz Prince
Sep WORLD WAR 3 ILLUSTRATED #36: NEO CONS (distributed)
Oct SUPERF*CKERS #2 by James Kochalka
Oct CONVERSATION #2 by James Kochalka & Jeffrey Brown

Oct 2nd Printing of BE A MAN by Jeffrey Brown
Nov COMIC BOOK ARTIST (VOL 2) #6: THE WILL EISNER ISSUE
Nov THE SURROGATES #3 (of 5) by Robert Venditti & Brett Weldele

2004

Jan VOICE OF THE FIRE by Alan Moore & José Villarubia, Intro by Gaiman
Jan VOICE OF THE FIRE (Signed Edition)
Jan THE OCTOPI & THE OCEAN by Dan James
Jan HAPPY #4: FEMALE by Josh Simmons
Feb THE SKETCHBOOK DIARIES (VOL 4) by James Kochalka
Feb JENNIFER DAYDREAMER #2: ANNA AND EVA by J. Daydreamer
Feb BE A MAN by Jeffrey Brown — 100th Official Publication!
Feb UPSIDE DOWN by Tobias Tak
Mar 3rd Printing of BLANKETS by Craig Thompson
Mar 5th Printing of GOOD-BYE, CHUNKY RICE by Craig Thompson
Mar GOOD-BYE CHUNKY RICE (Hardcover) by Craig Thompson
Mar VAN HELSING'S NIGHT OFF by Nicolas Mahler
Mar WARBURGER by Stripburger (distributed)
Mar COMIC BOOK ARTIST (VOL 2) #3 Edited by Jon B. Cooke
Apr 6th Printing of FROM HELL by Moore & Campbell
Apr 3rd Printing of CLUMSY by Jeffrey Brown
Apr TROGLODYTES by Marcel Ruijters
May THE MIRROR OF LOVE by Alan Moore & José Villarrubia
May THE MIRROR OF LOVE (Signed Edition)
May SAME DIFFERENCE & OTHER STORIES by Derek Kirk Kim
May ALL FLEE! by Gavin Burrows and Simon Gane
May DANG! by Martin Cendreda
Jun TOP SHELF TALES (FREE COMIC BOOK DAY)
Jun 2 SISTERS by Matt Kindt
Jun LESS THAN HEROES by David Yurkovich
Jun WORLD WAR 3 ILLUSTRATED #35: LIFE DURING WARTIME (distributed)
Jun HAPPY PACK by Josh Simmons
Jul CARNET DE VOYAGE by Craig Thompson
Jul AMERICAN ELF by James Kochalka
Jul AMERICAN ELF (Hardcover) by James Kochalka
Jul CONVERSATION #1: JAMES KOCHALKA & CRAIG THOMPSON
Jul BLANKETS SOUNDTRACK CD by Craig Thompson & Tracker
Aug GRAMPA & JULIE: SHARK HUNTERS by Jef Czekaj
Aug THE LEGEND OF WILD MAN FISCHER by Eichhorn & Williams
Sep OWLY (VOL 1): THE WAY HOME & THE BITTERSWEET SUMMER by Andy Runton
Sep DEAD HERRING COMICS by Actus (distributed)
Oct BIGHEAD by Jeffrey Brown
Oct COMIC BOOK ARTIST (VOL 2) #4 Edited by Jon B. Cooke
Dec HUTCH OWEN (VOL 2): UNMARKETABLE by Tom Hart
Dec COMIC BOOK ARTIST (VOL 2) #5 Edited by Jon B. Cooke

2003

Jan PISTOLWHIP (VOL 2): THE YELLOW MENACE by Matt Kindt & Jason Hall
Jan JENNIFER DAYDREAMER #1: OLIVER by Jennifer Daydreamer
Jan EGOMANIA #2: ALAN MOORE by Eddie Campbell (distributed)
Feb 2nd Printing of CLUMSY by Jeffrey Brown (1st Top Shelf Edition)

Feb MAGIC BOY & THE ROBOT ELF by James Kochalka
Feb 2nd Printing of CREATURE TECH by Doug TenNapel
Feb DEAR JULIA, SHORT FILM Directed by Alistair Banks Griffin (distributed)
Mar BEACH SAFARI by Mawil
Mar THE SKETCHBOOK DIARIES (VOL 3) by James Kochalka
Mar ALAN MOORE'S SNAKES & LADDERS CD
Apr MONKEY VS. ROBOT (VOL 2): THE CRYSTAL OF POWER by Kochalka
Apr HAPPY #3: ZIRKUS by Josh Simmons
Apr MADBURGER by Stripburger (distributed)
May TOP SHELF (#9): ASKS THE BIG QUESTIONS Edited by Brett Warnock & Rob Goodin
May ALAN MOORE LITHOGRAPH by José Villarrubia
May 4th Printing of GOOD-BYE, CHUNKY RICE by Craig Thompson
May APE POSTER by Craig Thompson
May ALAN MOORE: PORTRAIT OF AN EXTRAORDINARY GENTLEMAN by Millidge (distributed)
Jun THE MASTERPLAN by Scott Mills
Jun 2nd Printing of SKETCHBOOK DIARIES (VOL 1) by James Kochalka
Jul BLANKETS by Craig Thompson
Jul BLANKETS (Hardcover) by Craig Thompson
Jul UNLIKELY by Jeffrey Brown
Aug COMIC BOOK ARTIST (VOL 2) #1 Edited by Jon B. Cooke
Sep THE BAREFOOT SERPENT by Scott Morse
Sep THE BAREFOOT SERPENT (Hardcover) by Scott Morse
Sep WORLD WAR 3 ILLUSTRATED #34: TAKING LIBERTIES (distributed)
Sep MoCCA ART FESTIVAL POSTER Poster by Craig Thompson
Oct 2nd Printing of BLANKETS by Craig Thompson
Oct BOP! by Alex Robinson
Nov SHUCK UNMASKED by Rick Smith
Nov COMIC BOOK ARTIST (VOL 2) #2 Edited by Jon B. Cooke

2002
Jan HAPPY #1 by Josh Simmons
Jan Special 3rd Printing of GOOD-BYE, CHUNKY RICE by Craig Thompson
Feb BUGHOUSE (VOL 2): BAJA by Steve Lafler
Mar THE SKETCHBOOK DIARIES (VOL 2) by James Kochalka
Mar ALAN MOORE'S ANGEL PASSAGE CD
Apr STRIPBUREK by Stripburger (distributed)
May TRENCHES by Scott Mills
Jun PINKY & STINKY by James Kochalka
Jun DOUBLECROSS by Tony Consiglio
Jun XXX STRRIPBURGER by Stripburger (distributed)
Jun ALEC (VOL 4): AFTER THE SNOOTER by Eddie Campbell (distributed)
Jul THE 'K' CHRONICLES by Keith Knight
Jul HAPPY #2: ELEPHANT, BUNNY & CHICKEN by Josh Simmons
Jul EGOMANIA by Eddie Campbell (distributed)
Aug THREE FINGERS by Rich Koslowski
Aug LAND OF O by Michael Slack (distributed)
Sep CREATURE TECH by Doug TenNapel
Oct HAPPY END by Actus (distributed)
Oct 2nd Printing of MONKEY VS. ROBOT (VOL 1) by James Kochalka
Oct 2nd printing of BOX OFFICE POISON by Alex Robinson
Nov PINKY & STINKY MOCCA POSTER by Brett Warnock & James Kochalka
Dec WHERE HATS GO by Kurt Wolfgang (distributed)

2001

Jan BOY IN MY POCKET (BILLY DOGMA) by Dean Haspiel
Jan CIRKUS NEW ORLEANS by Josh Simmons
Feb SPEECHLESS by Peter Kuper
Mar HEY, MISTER #8: DIAL "M" FOR MISTER by Pete Sickman-Garner
Mar THE SKETCHBOOK DIARIES (VOL 1) by James Kochalka
Mar ALEC (VOL 3): HOW TO BE AN ARTIST by Eddie Campbell (distributed)
Apr BOX OFFICE POISON by Alex Robinson
May A COMPLETE LOWLIFE by Ed Brubaker
Jun THE SOAP LADY by Renée French
Jul PISTOLWHIP (VOL 1) by Matt Kindt & Jason Hall
Jul MEPHISTO by Matt Kindt & Jason Hall
Jul BETTER LUCK NEXT CENTURY by Dylan Horrocks
Jul SMUDGES by P. Shaw
Jul BERN & EDWINA by Pat Moriarity and David Greenburger
Aug THE ACTUS BOX: FIVE GRAPHIC NOVELLAS by Actus (distributed)
Aug ALEC (VOL 2): THREE PIECE SUIT by Eddie Campbell (distributed)
Sep SNAKES & LADDERS by Alan Moore & Eddie Campbell (distributed)
Oct MINIBURGER by Stripburger (distributed)
Nov ALAN MOORE'S THE HIGHBURY WORKING CD
Nov ABE: WRONG FOR ALL THE RIGHT REASONS by Glenn Dakin
Nov CICADA: A BROKEN FENDER BOOK by Josué Menjivar
Dec HEY, MISTER (VOL 3): THE FALL COLLECTION by Pete Sickman-Garner

2000

Feb DEAR JULIA, by Brian Biggs
Feb ALEC (VOL 1): THE KING CANUTE CROWD by Eddie Campbell (distributed)
Mar HEY, MISTER #6: THE TROUBLE WITH JESUS by Pete Sickman-Garner
May BUGHOUSE (VOL 1) by Steve Lafler
Jul FLIPPER (VOL 1) & FLIPPER (VOL 2) by Actus Tragicus (distributed)
Aug MONKEY VS. ROBOT (VOL 1) by James Kochalka
Aug DOOT DOOT GARDEN by Craig Thompson
Sep HEY, MISTER #7: EYES ON THE PRIZE by Pete Sickman-Garner
Sep BIBLE DOODLES by Craig Thompson
Nov BIG CLAY POT by Scott Mills
Dec HUTCH OWEN (VOL 1): THE COLLECTED by Tom Hart

1999

Jan TALES OF THE GREAT UNSPOKEN by Aaron Augenblick (distributed)
Feb SOFT SMOOTH BRAIN #2 by Bwana Spoons
Apr HEY, MISTER (VOL 2): CELEBRITY ROAST by Pete Sickman-Garner
May DAYDREAM LULLABIES (BILLY DOGMA) by Dean Haspiel
Jun THE BIRTH CAUL by Alan Moore & Eddie Campbell (distributed)
Jul THE PERFECT PLANET & OTHER STORIES by James Kochalka
Aug HEY, MISTER #5: BEHIND THE GREEN DOOR by Pete Sickman-Garner
Sep NEW HAT STORIES: BANKS/EUBANKS by Tom Hart
Oct GOOD-BYE, CHUNKY RICE by Craig Thompson
Nov FROM HELL by Alan Moore & Eddie Campbell
Dec TOP SHELF (#8): UNDER THE BIG TOP by Brett Warnock

1998
Feb TOP SHELF #6 Edited by Brett Warnock
Apr HEY, MISTER (VOL 1): AFTER SCHOOL SPECIAL by Pete Sickman-Garner
May BROKEN FENDER (VOL 2) #2 by Josué Menjivar
Jun CLOCK! #3 by Paul Sharar
Jun KEYHOLE #5 by Dean Haspiel & Josh Neufeld
Jul MAGIC BOY & GIRLFRIEND by James Kochalka
Aug HEY, MISTER #3 by Pete Sickman-Garner
Sep JACK'S LUCK RUNS OUT by Jason Little (distributed)
Nov TOP SHELF (#7): ON PARADE Edited by Brett Warnock
Dec HEY, MISTER #4 by Pete Sickman-Garner
Dec KEYHOLE #6 by Dean Haspiel & Josh Neufeld
1997
Mar EYE SPY by Charise Mericle
Jun THE STAROS REPORT — 1997 by Chris Staros
Jun PARANOIA by Kelly Hansen
Jul CRUST by Rick Pinchera
Aug TOP SHELF #5 Edited by Brett Warnock
Sep Chris Staros & Brett Warnock become partners in Top Shelf Productions, Inc. (18 September 1997)
Nov BROKEN FENDER (VOL 2) #1 by Josué Menjivar

1996
Mar I'M TOTALLY HELPLESS! by Wayne Shellabarger
Apr HURT ME! by Ulana Zahajkewycz
Apr TOP SHELF #2 Edited by Brett Warnock
Jul TOP SHELF #3 Edited by Brett Warnock
Aug GONE WALKABOUT by Steven Lewis Ryan
Sep MICROS by Paul Anson
Sep TOP SHELF #4 Edited by Brett Warnock

1995
Dec THE STAROS REPORT — 1996 by Chris Staros
Dec TOP SHELF #1 Edited by Brett Warnock
Dec DADDY DONNIE by Daniel-Patrick Evarts
Dec COLOR RIGHT by Charise Mericle

1994
Mar THE STAROS REPORT #1 by Chris Staros (Chris's debut)
Jun STREAM OF (UN)CONSCIOUSNESS by Brett Warnock (Brett's debut)
Oct THE STAROS REPORT #2 by Chris Staros

APPENDIX III:
TOP SHELF PUBLICATIONS BY CREATOR

This list covers everything that Chris Staros and Brett Warnock published separately and together, starting in March 1994 (with *THE STAROS REPORT #1*) and through December 2007. TOP SHELF PRODUCTIONS was originally called PRIMAL GROOVE PRESS, so all books published by Brett Warnock between 06/94 and 03/97 were published under that name. In 06/97, Brett changed the company name to TOP SHELF PRODUCTIONS, and in 09/07 (actually September 18th 1997, at the SPX) Chris pitched combining forces to Brett, and the new Top Shelf Productions was formed with a handshake. The first use of the Top Shelf logo was on *BROKEN FENDER (Vol 2) #1* (10/97), and the company officially became a corporation in 05/98.

Paul Anson
MICROS (Box of minis, $10.00, 09/96) out of print

Brian Biggs
DEAR JULIA, (graphic novel, $12.95, 02/00)
DEAR JULIA SHORT FILM (short film VHS, $15.00, 02/03)

Jeffrey Brown
CLUMSY (graphic novel, $10.00, 1st Top Shelf edition (2nd printing): 02/03, 2nd TSP (3rd): 04/04, 3rd TSP (4th): 07/05, 4th TSP (5th): 09/06)
UNLIKELY (graphic novel, $14.95, 1st printing: 07/03, 2nd: 07/05, 3rd: 05/07)
BE A MAN (comic book, $3.00, 1st printing: 02/04, 2nd: 10/05)
TOP SHELF TALES: FREE COMIC BOOK DAY BOOK 2004 (comic book, 32 pages, 06/04)
BIGHEAD (graphic novel, $12.95, 10/04)
MINISULK (graphic novel, $8.00, 03/05)
AEIOU (graphic novel, $12.00, 1st: 06/05, 2nd: 09/07)
CONVERSATION #2 (comic book w/James Kochalka, $4.95, 10/05)
EVERY GIRL IS THE END OF THE WORLD FOR ME (graphic novel, $8.00, 04/06)
I AM GOING TO BE SMALL (grahic novel, $14.00, 07/06)
FEEBLE ATTEMPTS (CB, Jeffrey Brown, $5.00, 03/07)
INCREDIBLE CHANGE-BOTS (full-color graphic novel, $15.00, 07/07)
INCREDIBLE CHANGE-BOTS (hardcover, $30.00, 07/07)

Ed Brubaker
A COMPLETE LOWLIFE (graphic novel, $12.95, 05/01)

Gavin Burrows & Simon Gane
ALL FLEE! (comic book, $3.95, 05/04)

Lilli Carré
TALES OF WOODSMAN PETE (graphic novel, $7.00, 06/06)

Martin Cendreda
DANG! (comic book, $3.50, 05/04)

Tony Consiglio
DOUBLECROSS (comic book, $4.95, 06/02)
110PER¢ (graphic novel, $12.95, 05/06)

Jon B. Cooke (editor)
COMIC BOOK ARTIST (VOL 2) #1 (magazine, $7.50, 08/03)
COMIC BOOK ARTIST (VOL 2) #2 (magazine, $7.50, 11/03)
COMIC BOOK ARTIST (VOL 2) #3 (magazine, $7.50, 03/04)
COMIC BOOK ARTIST (VOL 2) #4 (magazine, $7.50, 10/04)
COMIC BOOK ARTIST (VOL 2) #5 (magazine, $7.50, 12/04)
COMIC BOOK ARTIST (VOL 2) #6 (magazine, $14.50, 12/05)

Jef Czekaj
GRAMPA & JULIE: SHARK HUNTERS (graphic novel, $14.95, 08/04)

Glenn Dakin
ABE: WRONG FOR ALL THE RIGHT REASONS (trade paperback, $14.95, 11/01)

Jennifer Daydreamer
JENNIFER DAYDREAMER #1: OLIVER (comic book, $4.95, 01/03)
JENNIFER DAYDREAMER #2: ANNA AND EVA (comic book, $4.95, 02/04)

Dennis P. Eichhorn & J.R. Williams
THE LEGEND OF WILD MAN FISCHER (graphic novel, $7.95, 09/04)

Max Estes
HELLO, AGAIN (graphic novel, $10.00, 03/05)
COFFEE & DONUTS (graphic novel, $10.00, 02/06)

Daniel-Patrick Evarts
DADDY DONNIE (mini, $2.00, 12/95)

Renée French
THE SOAP LADY (hardcover children's book, $19.95, 07/01)
THE TICKING (hardcover graphic novel, $19.95, 04/06)
MICROGRAPHICA (graphic novel, $10.00, 05/07)

Kelly Hansen
PARANOIA (comic book, $10.00, 06/97) out of print

Tom Hart
NEW HAT STORIES: BANKS/EUBANKS (graphic novel, $9.95, 09/99)
HUTCH OWEN (VOL 1): THE COLLECTED (graphic novel, Vol 1, $14.95, 12/00)
HUTCH OWEN (VOL 2): UNMARKETABLE (graphic novel, Vol 2, $14.95, 11/04)

Andy Hartzell
FOX BUNNY FUNNY (graphic novel, $10.00, 06/07)

Dean Haspiel
DAYDREAM LULLIBIES: A BILLY DOGMA EXPERIENCE (trade paperback, $7.95, 05/99)
BOY IN MY POCKET: A BILLY DOGMA EXPERIENCE (comic book, $2.95, 01/01)

Dean Haspiel & Josh Neufeld
KEYHOLE #5 (comic book, $2.95, 06/98)
KEYHOLE #6 (comic book, $2.95, 12/98)

Dylan Horrocks
BETTER LUCK NEXT CENTURY (small batch comic book, $7.00, 07/01) out of print

Dan James
THE OCTOPI & THE OCEAN (comic book, $6.95, 01/04)
MOSQUITO (graphic novel, $12.95, 04/05)

Matt Kindt
2 SISTERS (graphic novel $19.95, 06/04)
SUPER SPY (graphic novel, $19.95, 08/07)
SUPER SPY (hardcover, $40.00, 08/07)

Matt Kindt & Jason Hall
MEPHISTO (comic book, $3.95, 07/01)
PISTOLWHIP (VOL 1) (graphic novel, $14.95, 07/01)
PISTOLWHIP (VOL 2): THE YELLOW MENACE (graphic novel, $14.95, 01/03)

Derek Kirk Kim
SAME DIFFERENCE & OTHER STORIES (graphic novel, $12.95, 1st Top Shelf edition:
        06/04, 2nd: 06/05)

Keith Knight
THE K CHRONICLES: WHAT A LONG STRANGE STRIP IT'S BEEN (trade paperback,
        $12.95, 07/02)

James Kochalka
MAGIC BOY & GIRLFRIEND (graphic novel, $8.95, 07/98) out of print
THE PERFECT PLANET & OTHER STORIES (graphic novel, $14.95, 07/99)
MONKEY VS. ROBOT (VOL 1) (graphic novel, $14.95, 1st printing: 08/00, 2nd: 10/02, 3rd
        (new edition): 05/05)
JAMES KOCHALKA'S SKETCHBOOK DIARIES (VOL 1) (comic book, $7.95, 1st printing:
        03/01, 2nd: 06/03)
JAMES KOCHALKA'S SKETCHBOOK DIARIES (VOL 2) (comic book, $7.95, 03/02)
PINKY & STINKY (graphic novel, $17.95, 06/02)
MAGIC BOY & THE ROBOT ELF (graphic novel, $9.95, 02/03)
JAMES KOCHALKA'S SKETCHBOOK DIARIES (VOL 3) (comic book, $7.95, 03/03)
MONKEY VS. ROBOT (VOL 2): THE CRYSTAL OF POWER (graphic novel, $14.95, 04/03)
JAMES KOCHALKA'S SKETCHBOOK DIARIES (VOL 4) (comic book, $7.95, 02/04)

TOP SHELF TALES: FREE COMIC BOOK DAY BOOK 2004 (comic book, 32 pages, 06/04)
AMERICAN ELF (BOOK1) (graphic novel, $29.95, 07/04)
AMERICAN ELF (BOOK 1) HC (hardcover, $50.00, 1st printing of 500 copies: 07/04)
CONVERSATION #1 (comic book w/Craig Thompson, $4.95, 07/04)
SUPERF*CKERS #1 (comic book, $7.00, 05/05)
SUPERF*CKERS #2 (comic book, $5.00, 10/05)
CONVERSATION #2 (comic book w/Jeffrey Brown, $4.95, 10/05)
SUPERF*CKERS #3 (comic book, $5.00, 06/06)
AMERICAN ELF (BOOK 2) (full-color graphic novel, $19.95, 02/07)
SUPERF*CKERS #4 (comic book, $5.00, 05/07)

Rich Koslowski
THREE FINGERS (graphic novel, $14.95, 08/02)
THE KING (graphic novel, $19.95, 07/05)
THE KING HARDCOVER (hardcover, $39.95, 07/05)

Peter Kuper
SPEECHLESS (full-color hardcover, $19.95, 02/01)

Steve Lafler
BUGHOUSE (VOL 1) (graphic novel, $14.95, 05/00)
BUGHOUSE (VOL 2): BAJA (graphic novel Steve Lafler, $9.95, 02/02)
BUGHOUSE (VOL 3): SCALAWAG (graphic novel Steve Lafler, $12.95, 04/05)

Jeff Lemire
ESSEX COUNTY (VOL 1): TALES FROM THE FARM (graphic novel, $9.95, 03/07)
ESSEX COUNTY (VOL 2): GHOST STORIES (graphic novel, $14.95, 09/07)

Nicolas Mahler
VAN HELSING'S NIGHT OFF (graphic novel, $12.95, 03/04)
LONE RACER (graphic novel, $12.95, 12/06)

Mawil
BEACH SAFARI (graphic novel, $9.95, 03/03)

Josué Menjivar
BROKEN FENDER (VOL 2) #1 (comic book, $2.95, 11/97)
BROKEN FENDER (VOL 2) #2 (comic book, $2.95, 06/98)
CICADA (graphic novel, $12.95, 11/01)

Charise Mericle
COLOR RIGHT (mini, $2.00, 12/95)
EYE SPY (comic book, $5.00, 1st printing: 03/97, 2nd printing: 08/98)

Scott Mills
BIG CLAY POT (graphic novel, $12.95, 11/00)
TRENCHES (graphic novel, $14.95, 05/02)
THE MASTERPLAN (graphic novel, $24.95, 06/03)

Alan Moore & Eddie Campbell
FROM HELL (graphic novel, $35.00, 1st Top Shelf edition: 05/04, 2nd: 08/06, 3rd: 05/07)

Alan Moore & José Villarrubia
ALAN MOORE LITHOGRAPH (lithograph, $40.00 signed [500], $20.00 unsigned, 05/03)
VOICE OF THE FIRE (hardcover novel, $26.95, 01/04)
VOICE OF THE FIRE (signed & numbered edition [500], $49.95, 01/04)
THE MIRROR OF LOVE (full-color hardcover, $24.95, 05/04)
THE MIRROR OF LOVE (signed & numbered edition [500], $24.95, 05/04)

Alan Moore & Melinda Gebbie
LOST GIRLS (Three 112-pg full-color hardcovers in a slipcase, $75.00, 1st: 08/06, 2nd:
        10/06, 3rd: 01/07)

Pat Moriarity & David Greenberger
BERN & EDWINA (small batch comic book, $7.00, 07/01)

Scott Morse
THE BAREFOOT SERPENT (graphic novel, $14.95, 09/03)
THE BAREFOOT SERPENT HARDCOVER (hardcover, $30.00, 09/03)
TOP SHELF TALES: FREE COMIC BOOK DAY BOOK 2004 (comic book, 32 pages, 06/04)

Rick Pinchera
CRUST (comic book, $3.00, 1st printing: 07/97, 2nd printing: 02/98) out of print

Nate Powell
PLEASE RELEASE (comic book, $3.95, 11/06)

Liz Prince
WILL YOU STILL LOVE ME IF I WET THE BED? (graphic novel, $7.00, 09/05)

Aaron Renier
TOP SHELF TALES: FREE COMIC BOOK DAY BOOK 2004 (comic book, 32 pages, 06/04)
SPIRAL-BOUND (graphic novel, $14.95, 08/05)

Alex Robinson
BOX OFFICE POISON (graphic novel, $29.95, 1st printing: 04/01, 2nd: 10/02, 3rd
        (new edition): 08/05, 4th: 01/06)
BOX OFFICE POISON HARDCOVER (hardcover, $49.95, 1st printing: 08/05)
BOP! (graphic novel, $9.95, 10/03)
TRICKED (graphic novel, $19.95, 1st printing: 08/05)
TRICKED HARDCOVER (hardcover, $39.95, 1st printing: 08/05, 2nd: 12/05)
LOWER REGIONS (comic book, $5.00, 11/07)

Marcel Ruijters
TROGLODYTES (graphic novel, $9.95, 05/04)

Andy Runton
OWLY (VOL 1): THE WAY HOME & THE BITTERSWEET SUMMER (graphic novel, $10.00,
        09/04, 2nd: 02/06, 3rd 01/08)
OWLY (VOL 2): JUST A LITTLE BLUE (graphic novel, $10.00, 1st: 02/05; 2nd: 09/06)
OWLY: SPLASHIN' AROUND (FREE COMIC BOOK DAY) (comic book, FREE, 05/05)
OWLY (VOL 3): FLYING LESSONS (graphic novel, $10.00, 1st: 12/05, 2nd: 04/07)
OWLY: BREAKIN' THE ICE (FREE COMIC BOOK DAY) (comic book, FREE, 05/05)
OWLY T-SHIRTS (big 700 T-Shirt Solicitation and Run, 03/06, continued reprints)
OWLY: BREAKIN' THE ICE (FCBD) (comic book, FREE, 05/06)
OWLY PLUSH TOY (Plush Toy, $19.95, 10/06)
OWLY: HELPING HANDS & KORGI: SPROUT'S LOST COOKIE (FCBD) (comic book,
        FREE, 05/05/07)
OWLY (VOL 4): A TIME TO BE BRAVE (graphic novel, $10.00, 12/07)
OWLY (VOL 4): A TIME TO BE BRAVE (hardcover, $20.00, 12/07)
OWLY (VOL 1): THE WAY HOME & THE BITTERSWEET (hardcover, $20.00, 12/07)

Steven Lewis Ryan
GONE WALKABOUT (comic book, $3.00, 08/96)

Paul Sharar
CLOCK! #3 (comic book, $2.95, 06/98)

P. Shaw
SMUDGES (small batch comic book, $7.00, 07/01)

Wayne Shellabarger
I'M TOTALLY HELPLESS! (comic book, $5.00, 03/96)

Pete Sickman-Garner
HEY, MISTER (VOL 1): AFTER SCHOOL SPECIAL (trade paperback of minis, $7.95,
        1st printing: 04/98, 2nd printing: 02/01)
HEY, MISTER #3 (comic book, $2.95, 08/98)
HEY, MISTER #4 (comic book, $2.95, 12/98)
HEY, MISTER (VOL 2): CELEBRITY ROAST (trade paperback #1 - #4, $9.95, 04/99)
HEY, MISTER #5: BEHIND THE GREEN DOOR (comic book, $2.95, 08/99)
HEY, MISTER #6: THE TROUBLE WITH JESUS (comic book, $2.95, 03/00)
HEY, MISTER #7: EYES ON THE PRIZE (comic book, $2.95, 09/00)
HEY, MISTER #8: DIAL 'M' FOR MISTER (comic book, $3.50, 03/01)
HEY MISTER (VOL 3): THE FALL COLLECTION (trade paperback #5 - #8, $12.95, 01/02)

Timothy Sievert
THAT SALTY AIR (graphic novel, $10.00, 12/07)

Josh Simmons
CIRKUS NEW ORLEANS (small batch comic book, $7.00, 02/01) out of print
HAPPY #1 (4-issue miniseries, $3.50, 01/02)
HAPPY #2: ELEPHANT, BUNNY & CHICKEN (4-issue miniseries, $3.50, 07/02)
HAPPY #3: ZIRKUS (4-issue miniseries, $3.50, 04/03)
HAPPY #4: FEMALE (4-issue miniseries, $3.50, 01/04)

Christian Slade
KORGI (BOOK 1): SPROUTING WINGS! (graphic novel, $10.00, 04/07)
KORGI (BOOK 1): SPROUTING WINGS! (hardcover, $20.00, 04/07)
OWLY: HELPING HANDS & KORGI: SPROUT'S LOST COOKIE (FCBD) (comic book, FREE, 05/05/07)

Rick Smith & Tania Menesse
SHUCK UNMASKED (graphic novel, $14.95, 11/03)

Bwana Spoons
SOFT SMOOTH BRAIN #2 (comic book, $3.00, 02/99)

Chris Staros
THE STAROS REPORT #1 (mini, $1.00, 03/94)
THE STAROS REPORT #2 (mini, $2.00, 10/94)
THE STAROS REPORT — 1996 (magazine, $4.95, 12/95)
THE STAROS REPORT — 1997 (magazine, $4.95, 06/97)
YEARBOOK STORIES: 1976-1978 (comic book, $4.00, 10/07)

Doug TenNapel
CREATURE TECH (graphic novel, $14.95, 1st printing: 09/02, 2nd: 02/03, 3rd: 01/05)

Craig Thompson
GOOD-BYE, CHUNKY RICE (graphic novel, $14.95, 1st printing: 10/99, 2nd: 02/01, 3rd: 01/02, 4th: 05/03, 5th: 03/04, 6th 01/05)
DOOT DOOT GARDEN (small batch comic book, $7.00, 1st printing: 08/00, 2nd: 02/01, 3rd: 07/01) out of print
BIBLE DOODLES (small batch comic book, $7.00, 1st printing: 09/00, 2nd: 02/01, 3rd: 07/01) out of print
BLANKETS (graphic novel, $29.95, 1st printing: 07/03, 2nd: 10/03, 3rd: 03/04, 4th: 10/04, 5th: 02/05, 6th: 12/05, 7th: 10/06, 8th: 05/07)
BLANKETS HARDCOVER (hardcover, $75.00, 1st printing of 500 copies: 07/03) out of print
GOOD-BYE, CHUNKY RICE HARDCOVER (hardcover, $29.95, 1st printing of 500 copies: 03/04)
CARNET DE VOYAGE (graphic novel, $14.95, 07/04, 2nd: 12/05)
CONVERSATION #1 (comic book w/James Kochalka, $4.95, 07/04)
THE BLANKETS SOUNDTRACK BY TRACKER (music CD, $15.00, 07/04)

Jeremy Tinder
CRY YOURSELF TO SLEEP (graphic novel, $7.00, 05/06)
BLACK GHOST APPLE FACTORY (graphic novel, $5.00, 07/07)

Robert Venditti & Brett Weldele
THE SURROGATES #1 (OF 5) (comic book, $2.95, 07/05)
THE SURROGATES #2 (OF 5) (comic book, $2.95, 09/05)
THE SURROGATES #3 (OF 5) (comic book, $2.95, 12/05)
THE SURROGATES #4 (OF 5) (comic book, $2.95, 01/06)
THE SURROGATES #5 (OF 5) (comic book, $2.95, 03/06)
THE SURROGATES 1.0 (graphic novel, $19.95, 07/06)

Brett Warnock (editor)
STREAM OF (UN)CONSCIOUSNESS (mini, $1.00, 1st printing: 06/94, 2nd printing: 12/95)
TOP SHELF #1 (anthology, $5.00, 12/95)
TOP SHELF #2 (anthology, $5.00, 04/96)
TOP SHELF #3 (anthology, $5.00, 07/96)
TOP SHELF #4 (anthology, $5.00, 09/96) out of print
TOP SHELF #5 (anthology, $6.95, 08/97)
TOP SHELF #6 (anthology, $6.95, 02/98)
TOP SHELF #7: ON PARADE (anthology, $6.95, 11/98)
TOP SHELF #8: UNDER THE BIG TOP (anthology, $14.95, 12/99)
TOP SHELF #9: ASKS THE BIG QUESTIONS (anthology, $24.95, 05/03)
        features Alan Moore & Melinda Gebbie's COBWEB story banned by DC Comics

David Yurkovich
LESS THAN HEROES (graphic novel, $14.95, 06/04)
DEATH BY CHOCOLATE: REDUX (graphic novel, $14.95, 06/07)

Ulana Zahajkewycz
HURT ME! (mini, $2.00, 04/96)

Aleksandar Zograf
REGARDS FROM SERBIA (graphic novel, $19.95, 01/07)

Cocktail party invitation art. Jeremy Tinder.

welcome to essex county

Promotional art for the Essex County Trilogy. Jeff Lemire

Tales From The Farm MARCH 2007   Ghost Stories SEPTEMBER 2007   The Country Nurse 2008

TOP

Art by Max Estes.

SHELF

Art by Max Estes.